THE

GOSPEL

OF THE

PHOENIX

STEPHEN H. PROVOST

To my mother, who showed me how to rise from the ashes.

Contents

"Many have undertaken to draw up an account of the things that have been believed among us, just as they were handed down to us by those who from the first were eyewitnesses and servants of the word. Therefore, since I myself have carefully investigated everything from the beginning, it seemed good also to me to write an orderly account for you ..." - Luke 1:1-2

Preface

When I first read the words on the previous page, from the Gospel of Luke, I was struck by their honesty. Here was someone who admitted he wasn't a first-hand witness to the events he described. He admitted his work was the result of his own inquiry, based on multiple sources "handed down" to him and then arranged in an orderly account.

Interestingly enough, this is exactly what scholars think

happened. Sayings attributed to Jesus were circulating for some time and were eventually written down in collections similar to Gospel of Thomas, a largely Gnostic document that includes 113 sayings ascribed to Jesus. During the same period, stories about signs and wonders attributed to Jesus also were circulating. These materials were used by authors as source materials for what we know as "gospels" – stories of Jesus' life.

Different authors assembled these pieces differently. The author of John, for instance, put Jesus' "cleansing of the temple" near the beginning of his account, whereas others put it (more reasonably, it would seem) close to the end. Accounts such as miraculous feedings were duplicated. One author placed a famous discourse on a "mount", another on a plain.

Moreover, each author included his own observations and commentary. On several occasions, the author of Matthew points out that something was done to fulfill a particular passage of Jewish scripture. The author of John, meanwhile, takes it upon himself to refute a rumor that one of the disciples would never die.

Each author had a different purpose, reflected in the content of his work. While Matthew emphasizes the fulfillment of prophecy, John focuses on the divinity of Jesus. Each author chose different pieces of tradition to achieve his specific purpose, not paying too much attention to such details as chronology or setting. To illustrate their points, they even borrowed from much older stories that were circulating in the region at that time about such demigods as Horus, Mithras, Dionysus and Krishna – stories that, in some cases, are transplanted faithfully into the gospel accounts. Turning water into wine ... being born in a manger ... dying and rising from the dead. ...

Moreover, some sayings are very similar to earlier aphorisms attributed to such sages as Hillel, Confucius and Gautama Buddha.

So the gospel accounts were attempts to create "orderly accounts" from at least four kinds of material: sayings and parables, stories of signs and wonders, material drawn from popular mythology, and the authors' own commentary.

As you may have noticed, I've used the phrases "attributed to" and "ascribed to" on several occasions. Such phrases can certainly be applied to the authors of the gospels themselves, none of whom name themselves in the texts. Rather, the names were added later based on a custom of the day: attributing a work to a famous or respected figure to give it an air of legitimacy. Today, we'd call that dishonest. At the time, it was done as a matter of course. Any number of manuscripts were attributed to Solomon (odes, psalms, songs, etc.) because he was widely revered as the wisest man who ever lived. His name added a sense of importance to any writings to which it was attached. Another example is Moses, who was said to have written the Torah – the first five books of the Hebrew scripture – despite the fact that these writings refer directly to his death.

Few experts believe that Solomon or Moses wrote the books that bear their names, and the same can be said for the anonymous writers of the gospels. Particularly absurd is the idea that Matthew, a supposed eyewitness to Jesus' life, should have built his work around the writings of Mark, someone who either never or barely knew him. Scholars are nearly unanimous, however, that large sections of Matthew (the book) were borrowed whole cloth from Mark.

The gospel writings we have today, therefore, are a hodgepodge of material assembled not by apostles but by "ghost writers" using sources with varying degrees of credibility. One group of scholars went so far as to scrupulously analyze the sayings of Jesus, discounting many of them as derivative, inconsistent or blatantly counterfeit. The point here is not to disparage the gospel accounts, but to view them for what they are: not a monolithic stone tablet of "truth" but a patchwork of writings by humans cobbled together from any number of sources. Their writers were not historians by any stretch of the imagination. They were poets and storytellers, following the conventions of their day. Their goal wasn't to present a historically accurate picture of the events they were relating, but rather to tell an engaging story that would encourage people to "believe" – not by facts, but by faith. Indeed, the author of John went so far as to state this goal explicitly, ascribing the following words to Jesus: "You believe because you have seen, but blessed are those who believe without seeing."

The goal was faith, not historical accuracy. And this is a goal they achieved beyond, perhaps, their wildest hopes. Faith doesn't require facts, but only an object on which to focus. The proof behind the visions of the Revelation, or Edgar Cayce for that matter, lies not in the realm of history, but in the realm of faith and poetry. The same may be said for the sacred books of Joseph Smith's church, the Aquarian Gospel of Jesus Christ and many other works, including the present volume. Is it sacrilege to place the biblical writings on the same level as these others? Not at all, when one considers how and by whom they were assembled.

This present volume is one such work. It makes expansive use of historical documents from a variety of sources, just as the gospel writers did. But these documents, like those Luke's author utilized, were not themselves written by historians. What follows is meant as a vehicle for insight, inspiration and personal understanding. Indeed, that's the stuff of magic. And the things described here can be considered nothing less than magical.

1

[1] When there was nothing
    Still there was truth
    Abiding in silence
    Not knowing itself

[2] And there abode wisdom,
    A bride to her bridegroom
[3] Saying, "Come my beloved,
    And let us be one."

[4] Her words of love birthing renewal in all things
    A song of creation

Eternally sung
⁵ One thought manifesting in all of the earth
A manifold tapestry
Ever new spun

⁶ Adorning the bride with fine jewels of great splendor
The gold of the sunrise
The emerald forests
The great lapis oceans
The silvery moonlight

⁷ For thought became deed
And word became substance
⁸ And took for its dwelling
The mouths of the sages
The song of the night bird
The dome of the heavens
The heart of the poor

⁹ Echoing down through the ages from wisdom
Love is eternal
All things are one

Selah

¹⁰ Now the great wheel spun an illusion called time, and all the earth became snared in its gossamer strands.
¹¹ And it spun forth an age of fire, when the earth was

hot and molten. ¹²In those days did fire rise up from the belly of the earth, ascending skyward in fountains of liquid gold. This was the first age.

¹³Then it spun an age of water, when great seas engulfed creation. ¹⁴Rain fell down and springs welled up, creating wide rivers and vast lakes. ¹⁵The mighty Nile sprang forth, and the great Euphrates. And mists hung over all the deep. This was the second age, the age of water.

¹⁶And the heavens were lifted away from the abyss, so that a cool wind swept away the lingering mist. ¹⁷The curtain of cloud was pulled away, and the sun's bright rays shone through. This was the third age, the age of air.

¹⁸Then the waters drew back from the face of the earth, yielding their place to barren deserts and great young mountains that rose up to touch the sky. ¹⁹The rivers carved out canyons, and caverns were crafted deep within the heart of the earth. This was the fourth age, the age of earth and stone.

²⁰Up from the depths of the underworld rose flowering plants of every sort, and ferns and palms, and cactus and mosses. ²¹Grasses covered the sweeping plain, and great trees that reached the height of a dozen men: the cedars of Lebanon, which gave shade to the blistered earth. This was the fifth age, the age of verdure.

²²Then at last there came a sixth age, which gave birth to the fish of the seas and the birds of the sky and the beasts of the field and the children of men. ²³This was the age of blood, a time of cruelty and striving, of desire and remorse.

^{24} And in their pride, the sons of men laid hold of wisdom, taking her by force from the garden she had planted east in Eden. She bestowed on them the power of speech, yet they in their arrogance sought to bind her with their words. ^{25} With vain decrees they held her fast. With scrolls and parchment, they made as if to contain her in their scriptures wrought by men.

^{26} Fools! Yet she confounded them.

^{27} She scattered their tongues four winds, so that no man understood his neighbor, and she fled from their sight like screech owl in the night. ^{28} They in their ignorance cursed her and said, "She is a demon!" And they named her Lilith. But children of the wise do call her Isis, queen of heaven, Aphrodite, Astarte, Venus, Inanna.

^{29} Therefore did the children of men forgot their beginnings and cast about in vain for understanding. ^{30} Their ears heard not the poet, and hearkened not to the wise ones. ^{31} Mistaking parable for chronicle, they made for themselves false histories, and these they used to justify their cruelty.

^{32} From their mouths sprang forth a cacophony of madness, each naming his gods by different names and seeking to assuage them with the blood of guileless creatures. ^{33} They waged war with one another and with the earth from which they had been taken, being called Adam, which means "earth."

^{34} So the gods withdrew from them also and left them to their folly.

The Coming of Osiris

[35] Yet still did wisdom visit men of virtue, abiding in the mouths of the sibyl and the healer, the sage and the seer. [36] She sent them the wise king Osiris, who ruled the two lands of Egypt with his consort, the lovely Isis. [37] It was he who brought the arts of learning and cultivation to the Nile lands, while she was skilled in wisdom and healing. Therefore was he called "gardener" and "teacher."

[38] Osiris had a brother called Set who coveted his throne. Therefore did he devise a scheme in treachery to

supplant wisdom's chosen king. [39] Crafting for himself a large ark of the finest wood, covered in gold and precious jewels, he waited until the day of a great feast in Egypt. This he presented to the guests there with this challenge: Whosoever should fit inside the box perfectly should claim it as his own.

[40] Set had fashioned the box in such a way that none save his brother would be able to enter it. [41] So each of the guests stepped forward one by one, yet none was able to meet the challenge. [42] Then at length did the turn pass to Osiris, whereupon he climbed inside and found it fit him perfectly! [43] Yet at that same moment, Set rushed forward with seventy-two of his disciples to seal the ark shut while the king reclined there. [44] With great alacrity did they make their escape, spiriting the ark away and casting it forth on the waters of the Nile, which now flowed swiftly as the tears of grieving Isis.

[45] Still, hope was not abandoned, for the queen used charms and magic to conceive a child in spirit by her fallen husband. And she named him Horus of the Horizon.

[46] And when Horus had grown to manhood, he avenged his father's death by slaying Set in mortal combat. [47] His sign is the falcon and the fiery sun, whose bark bears forth the wisest of Adam's children across the sky to life eternal. For Isis is the font of wisdom, and her son its true expression.

[48] The first upon whom she placed her blessing was called Enoch, whose very name means wisdom. He was taken up on the bark of Horus after abiding for 365 times,

so that he rode across the heavens with the sun in all its glory. [49] So it was also with Elijah and the rest whom Isis has so favored. Her dove came unto Noah. Through Solomon she spoke, and Hillel, and Gamaliel, and through Jesus and many others who had ears to hear her.

The Sayings of the Masters

[50] These therefore are her words, the sayings of the masters:

[51] "The way is a great mother, empty yet inexhaustible. She gives birth to worlds unending. Ever present within you, manifest her as you will."

[52] "No thing exists in solitude. All things stand in relation to every other thing."

[53] "The world is sacred in perfection. To disturb it is to spoil it. To possess it is to lose it."

[54] "As we think so also we are. All that we are arises with our thoughts. With our thoughts, we make the world."

[55] "The master watches the world around him, yet trusts the sight within. He permits all things to come and go. His heart is open to the sky."

[56] "To live a pure and selfless life, count nothing as your own in the midst of abundance."

[57] "Freedom may not be had by obtaining every desire, but by controlling all desire."

[58] "Holding to anger is like grasping a hot coal, seeking to hurl it at another. You are the one who is burned."

[59] "Give evil nothing to oppose, and it will vanish of its own accord."

[60] "Speak for those who have no voice, and for the rights of all who are destitute."

[61] "By three methods may one learn wisdom. By reflection, which is noblest. By imitation, which is easiest. And by experience, which is bitterest."

[62] "That which we wish, we are quick to believe. That which we think, we imagine others think as well."

[63] "No one can save us, but only ourselves. We ourselves must walk the path."

[64] "All war is based on deceit."

[65] "In the sky, there is no distinction between east and west. The children of men create distinctions in their own

minds, then believe them to be true."

⁶⁶ "He who does not increase, decreases."

⁶⁷ "No gem can be polished without friction, nor can a man be perfected without trial."

⁶⁸ "If you wish to lead them, learn how to follow."

⁶⁹ "Expectation is the greatest hindrance to living. While it anticipates the morrow, it loses today."

⁷⁰ "The master seeks not fulfillment. Neither seeking nor expecting, she is present and can welcome all things."

⁷¹ "Boast not of the morrow, for you know not what a day may bring."

⁷² "Like an earring of gold or a precious adornment is the wise man's rebuke in the ear that attends him."

⁷³ "It is better to travel well than to arrive."

⁷⁴ "Like clouds and wind without rain is the one who boasts of gives he does not give."

⁷⁵ "The hard and stiff shall be broken; the soft and supple shall prevail."

⁷⁶ "If you wish to be whole, let yourself be limited.

    If you wish to go straight, let your path be winding

    If you wish to be filled, let yourself be empty

    If you wish to be reborn, let yourself die

    If you wish to receive all things, release all things."

⁷⁷ "A soul is nourished by its kindness, but destroyed by its own cruelty."

⁷⁸ "What has been shall be again. What has been accomplished shall be done again. There is nothing new beneath the sun."

⁷⁹ "He who knows that all things change clings to

nothing."

⁸⁰ "As a dog returns to its vomit, so a fool returns to his folly."

⁸¹ "Hatred does not cease by hatred, but by love. This is the eternal rule."

⁸² "True perfection seems imperfect, yet is perfectly itself. True fullness seems empty, yet even so is fully present."

⁸³ "The desire of the sluggard will be the death of him, for his hands refuse to labor. All the day he craves for more, yet the virtuous give without sparing."

⁸⁴ "Know yourself."

⁸⁵ "God is the universal essence of all things. All things are contained in him. He is the fount of being. In him do all things exist."

⁸⁶ "Seeing into darkness is clarity. Knowing how to yield is strength. Use your own light and return again to the source of light. This is the way of eternity."

⁸⁷ These are the words of wisdom crying in the wilderness, seeking to restore her garden in the seventh age yet to come. ⁸⁸ In this, the age of spirit, time's illusion shall be shattered and all things will return to one. Then shall the people enter into their rest. And until that day, the word abides.

2

¹ These are the chronicles of the word manifested in hope from a son of man who spoke the word.

² Called by some Jesus, by others Yeshua, and by others yet Issa, he dwelt in an age now past but dwells among us still in word and remembrance.

³ Born in the last days of King Herod, he was called the bridegroom, heir to Solomon's throne of wisdom, who would rebuild a temple not made by human hands but through wisdom and understanding. For it is written:

⁴ Wisdom calls aloud in the street
    She raises her voice in the public squares

⁵ At the head of the noisy streets she cries out
  In the gateways of the city she makes her speech:
⁶ How long will you simple ones love your simple ways?
  How long will mockers delight in mockery
  And fools hate knowledge?
For those who have ears to hear, let them hear.

⁷ Now it came to pass in those days that Herod saw betrayal all about him. And he divorced Mariamne the Egyptian, also called Mary, because he believed her to be plotting against him. ⁸ Though she was the fairest woman in all the land, this was nothing in the face of his wrath, therefore did he send her away from him. ⁹ Yet this was not the worst of his transgressions. Becoming mad with rage, he ordered each of his sons executed one after another; only Mariamne's own son Philip escaped and in due course married a woman named Herodias.

  This daughter's name was Salome.

¹⁰ At this time also, Herod deposed Mary's father Simeon as high priest and replaced him with one from another family.

¹¹ When these things took place, it was almost three score years since the coming of the Romans, when the general Pompey entered the temple, desecrating it. ¹² Since those days, the sons of Rome had remained among us, subjecting us to their decrees and demanding heavy taxes to feed their treasuries. And Herod was their servant.

¹³ Now Mary was newly with child, and when it became known that she had borne a son, Herod feared that his

enemies would use the newborn against him. For this birth was being hailed as a miracle.

[14] Some say that he was born under a date palm tree, the sacred tree of the phoenix in Egypt; others, that he came forth from a cave, the womb of the great earth mother. [15] Still others say he was born in a stable and placed in a feeding trough with animals round about him. [16] As it was written: "The ox knows his master and the donkey his owner's manger, yet Israel does not know and my people do not understand."

[17] And again:

The wolf and lamb will abide together
 The leopard shall lie down beside the goat
 The calf and lion and yearling together
 And a little child shall lead them

[18] And Simeon himself came to the child and blessed him in the temple, proclaiming him to be the messiah. [19] Others, too were gathering to him, bestowing gifts upon the infant and offering him their service. [20] This, to Herod, was sufficient to stoke his wrath. So he had a rumor spread that the child was a son of fornication, being the offspring of a certain soldier named Pantera.

[21] And he sent forth spies to seek out mother and child, signing a decree that all newborn male children should be slaughtered.

[22] Yet Mary, having given birth, fled with her new husband to Egypt and hid the child there.

[23] For it is written:

> Do you come to kiss this child?
>   I will not let you kiss him
> [24] Do you come to soothe him?
>   I will not let you soothe him
> [25] Do you come to do him harm?
>   I will not let you harm him
> [26] Do you come to take him away?
>   I will not let you take him from me!

The Phoenix Reborn

[27] During their travels, they came to the temple in On, which is called Heliopolis, the City of the Sun in the heart

of Egypt, as foretold by the prophet Jeremiah. [28] It is said by some that Adam, known to the Egyptians as Atum, was created there.

[29] It is in Heliopolis that there dwell the sacred priests of the phoenix, that mystical bird which is consumed in a fire and reborn from its ashes. [30] The Egyptians say that it bears within its bosom the very soul of Osiris, the heavenly father, and that its appearance heralds the birth of a new king. And it takes upon itself a form like unto a heron.

[31] There was in Heliopolis a giant obelisk, upon which the phoenix was said to alight. And atop this was placed a sacred stone called the ben-ben, bearing a cross upon which the great bird would perch. [32] This was the stone spoken of by the psalmist who said, "The stone that the builders rejected has become the capstone," inasmuch as Jesus had been cast out of Israel but would after a time become lifted up as a light brighter than the sun for all to see.

[33] When he was in Egypt, all this was revealed by the priests of the city, who were wise in the ways of the heavens and of magic and philosophy. [34] These men had watched the skies for a sign, and had seen a bright star rise up from beneath the earth in the east: the star of Hor-em-akhet, lord of the Horizon and son of the heavenly father Osiris. [35] He it was who was reborn each year from beneath the earth to his mother, whose name was Isis. Yet she had another name, as well, which was Mery.

[36] Now when Mary arrived with her son Jesus, it was at the very time this star appeared. And for this reason, the

magi of Heliopolis took his arrival as a sign to them that Hor-em-akhet called Horus had come in the flesh. [37] As it was written in the ancient texts:

> "A youth sat in the presence of the universal lord
>   Claiming the office of his father, Osiris
> [38] Beautiful in appearance,
>   He illumines the west with his face
>   As Thoth presents the healthy eye
>   To the great prince in Heliopolis
> [39] Then said Shu, the son of Re,
>   In the presence of the great prince in Heliopolis
>   'Power is borne by Justice'
>   And 'Award the office to Horus!' "

[40] The magi of On relate this story of the phoenix,

which has come down to them through the ages: "There is a bird we call the benu, which is the only one of its kind. [41]And it passes during its lifetime five hundred years until, when it has come time for it to die, it makes a nest for itself of spice and frankincense and myrrh, and therein breathes its last."

[42] And for this reason, some began to say that magi from the east came forth to present these gifts to Jesus. [43] Yet in truth, these things never came to pass. For it was the magi of On who saw the star rising in the east, and who speak of frankincense and myrrh in their story of the phoenix. [44] Likewise, some said he was born under a date palm, because this tree in Egypt is called a benu, after the phoenix, and as with the phoenix that alights upon the cross, Jesus was likewise to be reborn. [45] And though his mother had taken to herself a new husband, it was said that Jesus was the son of a heavenly father, that is Osiris.

[46] So it was that Mary remembered all these things in her heart and told them to her son when he was of an age to understand them, and he listened and he told them to those that came after him. [47] "I tell you the truth," he would say to them, "no one shall see the realm of God unless he is born again."

Way of the Therapeutae

[48] Now Mary kept her son in Egypt, for it was foretold by the prophet Jeremiah: [49] "He will set fire to the temples of the gods in Egypt; he will set their temples afire and take

captive their gods. [50] As a shepherd wraps his garment around him, so he will wrap Egypt around himself and depart from there unscathed." [51] And all this came to pass, according to the prophecy. Jesus' very presence set the temples afire with excitement that Hor-em-akhet had returned, and the priests there kept him safe during his sojourn, so that he would indeed depart unscathed, taking captive to himself the wisdom of the gods of Egypt, which he would share at the appointed time.

[52] During these days, they passed by Alexandria, where dwelt the Therapeutae, whose mission was healing and seeking after wisdom. As it is written, "The tongue of the wise brings healing."

[53] The Therapeutae lived in harmony near the lake called Mareotis, with its brackish waters and reeds bending low round about. [54] There did they immerse themselves in the traditions handed down by their elders through generations, which they called the Theravada, meaning

"ancient teaching." [55] These things, it is said, were from the east, whence they came to spread the knowledge of the eternal spirit and denial of the self.

[56] They therefore self-called themselves "servants," disdaining the goods of the world and holding all things in common. [57] Not deeming it proper for a man to be placed above a woman, both were held in equal esteem and admitted to their common meetings. Many of the things they were teaching, Jesus also taught as well.

[58] The precepts of the Therapeutae were four in number. [59] First, that the essence of life is suffering, and then second, that its cause is desire. [60] Therefore, they said, could suffering be removed by renouncing all desire, the third precept. And the fourth was the pathway which leads to this end.

[61] It is for this reason that the Therapeutae shared all their possessions, thereby removing all cause for desire. Wherefore Jesus would admonish those who followed him: "Go, sell all you have, and give the money to those in need."

[62] For he told them, "Therefore I say to you, have no concern about your life and what you will eat or drink, or about your body and how to clothe it. Is not life more than food and the body more than garments?

[63] "Look to the birds of the air, which do not sow or reap or store away in barns, and yet their father in heaven feeds them. Will he not do the same for you? Who of you, by worrying, can add a single hour to his life?

[64] "And why should you worry about what you will

wear? Behold the lilies of the field, which neither labor nor do they spin. Yet I say to you, even Solomon in all his splendor was not arrayed as one of these. [65] If this is how God clothes the grass in the field, which is here today and tomorrow is fuel for the fire, will he not clothe you also?

[66] "Therefore have no care in saying, 'What shall we eat?' or 'What shall we drink?' or 'What shall we wear?' For the ignorant run after these things, which your father in heaven already knows that you need. [67] But seek first his realm and his way, and then all these things will be given to you in like manner. [68] Worry not for tomorrow, but let it worry for itself. Each day has enough trouble for his own."

[69] And this he told them because he knew that they would suffer, and he sought to show them the pathway from suffering into light.

[70] Yet he knew also that his own path must lead through suffering to enlightenment.

[71] He who has ears to hear, let him hear.

Wars and Rumors of War

[72] In the final days of Herod and thereafter, there arose in Judea and Galilee great strife and tumult. For Herod had begun to build a spectacular temple to the god of Israel, but defiled it with the image of the eagle, thus exalting the empire above heaven itself.

[73] In those days, certain men arose named Judas ben Ezekias of Sepphoris and Matthias ben Margalus who were vexed at the acts of Herod. They saw that he had grown ill

and feeble, and they were emboldened to oppose him.
[73] They therefore called upon the people to go forth and cut down the golden eagle from its place above the temple gate. Such men as were affected by their words went forth in full daylight and, using sturdy ropes, let themselves down from the height of the temple and laid axes to the image of the eagle.

[74] Herod, however, was not so infirm as they first supposed, and those under his command yet obeyed him for fear of his wrath. [75] When, therefore, news of these events reached the ear of the temple guard's captain, he made great haste with a full contingent of armed men to the site of the unrest. In due course, the soldiers under his command laid hands on forty of the young men, whom he brought to stand before the king.

[76] The men they had taken into custody, consumed by their zeal, confessed to their crime. Thereupon did Herod command that they be burned alive and that those who were with them be put to death, along with their teachers. [77] But Judas escaped and returned to Sepphoris, where he began laying plans for greater sedition.

[78] Before long, Herod was overtaken by a gross distemper that ravaged his limbs and organs. And, his mind being afflicted as well, he ordered a large number of citizens be locked inside the hippodrome, giving orders that they should be slain upon the news of his death. [79] In this way, he reasoned, though the whole country hated him, all would yet mourn upon his passing.

[80] These orders, however, were not carried out, so that

there was no mourning at Herod's demise, but the whole land celebrated. [81] Yet still his death did not bring to an end the strife that engulfed the land in those days, for his kingdom was divided among three of his sons, whose ways were no less cruel than their father's had been. Thus were the country's divisions magnified by their quarrels.

[82] In those days and the times that followed, the land was full of bandits and men who called themselves "messiah." [83] One among them, a certain shepherd named Athronges set himself up as king of the Jews, even daring to crown himself king. [84] He and his followers cut down a Roman centurion at Emmaus, and his rebellion continued for some two years before it was ended. As to what became of Athronges, no man knows.

[85] Another brigand, Simon of Perea, likewise set a diadem upon his head. He and his men burned the royal palace at Jericho before his ambitions were ended by Gratus, the captain of the royal infantry, who slew him in combat.

[86] Then also, Judas the Galilean, drew to himself a great number of followers, and these men invaded the royal armory at Sepphoris. This Judas and another man named Zadok, whose name means "righteous," raised a rebellion to protest the payment of taxes to Caesar, and thus began a movement that would persist for many years. [87] These were the Zealots, many of whom came forth from Galilee, where Jesus also made his home.

3

¹ When Jesus was but a child, King Herod breathed his
last, and his kingdom was divided among three of his heirs.
² To his son Archelaus the sovereign bequeathed the heart
of his kingdom, which is Judea, Idumea and Samaria. ³ And
though his followers proclaimed him king, Archelaus
declined such an honorific, bowing instead to the will of
Caesar Augustus and taking for himself the title of
ethnarch, which translated means leader of the nation. ⁴ His
half-brother Philip was granted the northeast territory
around Caesarea Philippi, which city he rebuilt and was
named in his honor. ⁵ And another half-brother, Antipas,
received charge of the Galilee.

⁶ Antipas, for his part, built the new city of Tiberias on
the southwest shore of Lake Gennesaret, known by some

as the Sea of Galilee (though in truth it was surrounded on all sides by land and barely large enough to be named a lake). [7] In antiquity, this place had been called Rakkat, but Antipas replaced this small village with a modern city, naming it in honor of the emperor's adopted son. [8] He also ruled over the city of Sepphoris, called Tzippori, the largest city in the region and a center of learning and commerce.

[9] Antipas and Philip each governed his own territory as a tetrarch, ruling under the auspices of Caesar for many years and living into their middle years and beyond. [10] Archelaus, however, was driven from his office barely ten years after receiving it, because the people raised a tumult against him. Caesar therefore banished him to Gaul and installed his own favorites, called prefects, to watch over Samaria, Judea and Idumea.

[11] About this time, Jesus came into the temple courts and began to question the priests and scholars there. They were amazed at his questions and the answers he gave to them. [12] But it is said that he left from there and went with the Therapeutae to the land of their birth, which is called Sind in the west of India.

Jesus in India

[13] In those days, merchants driving caravans carried goods from east to west, braving robbers and other dangers as they came from China and India along the great Silk Road. [14] This route runs to the end of the earth from Damascus, stretching across the land of the Parthians

through Ctesiphon and into the heart of India. [15] Thence came traders to the cities and outposts of the west, bringing with them silk and other treasures to exchange for gold in the western empires.

[16] It was in India that Jesus is said to have found refuge. There he dwelt among the laborers, merchants and artisans in that land. [17] But the priests and the scholars refused to allow him into their presence, for the merchants and artisans were not permitted to read the sacred texts. They were allowed only to hear such things on festival days, being otherwise restricted from these writings.

[18] Further, the priests said, those of the laboring class below them were not even permitted to hear or contemplate the words of the text, for it was their lot only to serve those in the classes above them.

[19] (Now the lowest class of all was the untouchables, who engaged in actions that were considered ritually impure. These were shunned in the same manner as lepers, who Jesus would take compassion on and minister to in their afflictions, so purifying them restoring them to the

fellowship of all men).

20 And the priests said to Jesus, "Death alone can free them from their servitude. Come, therefore, away from them and give honor to the gods."

21 But Jesus refused, saying, "The father makes no distinction among his children, for he holds them all equally dear."

22 In these days it is said that Jesus, who was called by that people Issa, traveled also to Persia and Nepal and the great heights of Tibet. 23 These are the mountains that bear the weight of all the heavens, as pillars support the roof of a great temple. Next to them, the mountain called Zion seemed but a pebble, and they seemed ever adorned in garments far whiter than the purest priestly robes. 24 As he passed this way, he learned for himself the ways of the Buddha, called Gautama, who had gone this way before him, and who had said to his followers: "We are the heirs of all our own actions."

25 Were these not the same things said also by Solomon, who had declared, "Cast your bread upon the waters, and it shall return to you"?

26 Yet in this land, such wisdom was known by the names of karma and vipaka, which translated mean "action" and "fruit." 27 No healthy tree could bear bad fruit, nor could a rotten tree produce a good harvest. Workers did not pick figs from thorn bushes or grapes from briars, did they? 28 In the same manner, the good man would bring forth good things out of the good that is found in his heart, and the evil man, in like manner, would spew out evil

things. For the mouth was the gatekeeper to the heart's abundance.

²⁹ These things Jesus took to his heart and remembered from his travels.

³⁰ So he taught his disciples according to this way:

³¹ "Blessed are the poor, for theirs is the realm of heaven.

³² "Blessed are the mourners, for they shall be comforted.

³³ "Blessed are the humble, for the earth is their inheritance.

³⁴ "Blessed are those who hunger and thirst for goodness, for they shall be filled.

³⁵ "Blessed are the pure in heart, for they shall see God.

³⁶ "Blessed are the peacemakers, for they shall be called God's children.

³⁷ "Blessed are they who are persecuted for their goodness, for the realm of heaven is theirs."

³⁸ These were the teachings of Jesus.

³⁹ "Is not God good and merciful, granting to his children all they need to live? What man, when asking his father for a fish, will be given a stone? Even more so will the heavenly father care for his children.

⁴⁰ "Therefore," he told them, "Ask! And it shall be given to you. Seek! And you shall find. Knock! And the door will be opened to you. ⁴¹ The one who seeks should not stop until he finds. And when he finds, he shall be grieved, yet when he is grieved, he shall marvel, and when he marvels, he shall be the master of all things. Then shall

he rest."

⁴² Now some did not understand these teachings, saying that, behold, the one who asks for riches will surely receive them. ⁴³ Yet what are riches? Are they gold and silver, jewels and possessions? Or are they riches found within? ⁴⁴ So Jesus would admonish the wealthy, "Go, and sell all you have, and give the money to the poor. Then will you be rich in heaven's realm. For man may not serve God and money, and it is a hard thing indeed for a rich man to enter God's realm."

⁴⁵ For those who have ears to hear, let them hear!

⁴⁶ During his travels, Jesus continue to amaze those who dwelt among the eastern lands with his wisdom. ⁴⁷ And he taught them concerning the nature of this world. ⁴⁸ For he said to them, "The world is a bridge. Pass over it, but do not settle upon it." And again, "The world is a proud house. Heed this well, and do not build on its foundations."

⁴⁹And he also said, "Become passers-by."

The Ten Methods

⁵⁰ He therefore taught those who were with him ten methods of contemplating the world and its ways.

⁵¹ "Know first that when the children of men are born, from that day they begin to grow old and will certainly die. ⁵² The world is like an inn, and you are only lodgers. The bed and the tables therein are not yours. Soon, you will pass beyond that place, for no one can tarry long at an inn.

[53] "See how your friends and loved ones are taken from you, just as leaves fall from a tree in autumn. When winter arrives, wind shakes the leaves from the branches, and they are gone.

[54] "In this world, the success of the mighty and the wealth of the rich man do not endure. They are like the moon at night, which casts its light on all things until the clouds appear, or until the moon begins to wane and its light is forgotten.

[55] "In this world, the children of men steal things from one another because they think them valuable, but at length will do them harm. They are drawn as moths to the light, but heedless, dive into the flame.

[56] "The wealthy use up both body and spirit in gathering treasures that will not benefit them in the end. They are like jars that cannot hold the rivers, lakes and seas they covet.

[57] "Consider the world, this place where the children of men seek to fulfill the desires of the flesh, yet gain only sorrow and are not fulfilled. They are like a tree infested by insects that sap its strength and consume its heart until it dries up and breaks.

[58] "In this world, the children of men become drunk so that they no longer see the good and the bad. They are like a clear pool in springtime, whose surface reflects all things perfectly like a mirror, but which becomes clouded with mud so that the images vanish, leaving filthy water in which nothing can be seen.

[59] "The children of this world act as though life is a game, and they sit idly for hours of the day as their spirit becomes drained. These are like a madman who imagines he has seen flowers, then stumbles around through the darkness, seeking them anew. In the end, he is exhausted and sees nothing.

[60] "The children of this world go from one path to the next seeking truth but find only confusion. They are like a master carpenter who carves wood in a certain way, then adorns it with color so that it resembles an ox. But when he takes it into the field to plow, it sits there and does nothing.

[61] "In this world, many seem to follow these ways, but deceive themselves and benefit no one. They are like an oyster that holds within it a bright pearl. A fisherman comes and breaks the shell to have the pearl, and the oyster dies. They are left with the beauty of the pearl and a dead oyster."

[62] And Jesus went forth having learned these things and

shared his wisdom with everyone he met.

4

¹ But it came to pass that, after a time, he returned to his homeland and settled in Galilee of the Gentiles. And he became known there as a sage and a worker of wonders.

² Some have said he was a carpenter, but these know not the meaning of the word that is so translated, for in truth he was a sage, and he built a reputation as a magus. ³ Such was his wisdom that it had not been seen since the days of Solomon.

⁴ And Jesus' mother gave birth to his brothers, who were named James and Simon and Judas and Joses. And these became his followers. ⁵ James was known as "the

Just," for he had taken a vow neither to drink nor to let any razor touch his hair. He wore not wool but linen, and he was called Oblias, which means "Bulwark of the People." [6] Simon was called Cephas or Peter, meaning "A Rock." He was quick of temper, for he was a zealot, believing with those who would establish a new kingdom by force of arms. [7] Judas was called as Thomas or Didymus, which means "the Twin," and was also called "the Knife-Wielder," for he was an assassin. [8] And Joses was also called John.

[9] About this time, some began to say that the kingdom had come to another man named John, who was baptizing in the river Jordan. His name means, "God is Gracious." [10] This man had set himself apart in the wilderness and had taken the vow of a Nazirite, neither shearing his hair nor tasting the fruit of the vine. [11] He was like a wild man of old, calling the people to him with great power like Samson the mighty or the prophet Elijah. And men were saying that, behold, Elijah had returned to walk among them.

[12] There were in those days men in that place called Essenes, who followed in the ways of their brethren the Therapeutae, holding all things in common and neither buying nor selling. [13] These had withdrawn from the world to live a life of poverty in the wilderness. They were also champions of freedom, laying down all weapons and practicing daily baptisms. [14] They lived in many places, but most especially in the desert at Qumran, whence John also came. [15] And his appearance greatly troubled many men, for here was one who spoke with a tongue hot as fire and

sharp like a steely blade.

The Circle-Drawer

[16] Now in times past had there been such a one, whose name was Honi, which also means "Gracious." [17] Honi was an Essene and a great wonder-worker, and he was said to have the ear of God, just as Elijah had before him. For as Elijah called down fire from heaven, so did Honi call down water from above.

[18] Once a terrible drought was upon the land of Israel, and no rains had fallen by the month of Adar, so the people sent word to Honi. [19] He prayed, but no rains came. So he drew for himself a circle on the face of the dusty earth and stood inside it, raising his arms up toward the heaven. And he declared to God, "Until you send forth rain, I shall not move from within this circle!"

[20] And at these words, there came forth from heaven a few drops of water, which hissed as they struck the hot stones. [21] But the people murmured that this was not enough, so Honi turned his face once more to heaven and spoke thus: "Not for this trifling drizzle have I asked, but for rain to fill wells and cisterns and ditches!"

[22] At once the heavens opened, and rain poured down in torrents as during the time of Noah, each drop that fell being enough to fill a soup ladle. [23] Wells and cisterns overflowed, and the wadis flooded the desert, so that the people scrambled for safety, running to the Temple Mount to avoid being swept away. [24] And they cried to Honi, "Save

us! Or we shall be destroyed like the generation of the great flood. Cause the rains to cease!"

²⁵ But Honi said to them, "I was glad to ask that God should end your misery, but how can I now ask him to end your blessing?"

²⁶ Still, they continued to beseech him until at last he agreed to petition God once more. And he said to God, "This people that you brought up out of Egypt can take neither too much evil nor too much good. Give them therefore what they ask for, that they may be fulfilled."

²⁷ Then a strong wind came and swept away the torrents of rain, and the people went to gather mushrooms and truffles on the Temple Mount.

²⁸ But the leader of the Sanhedrin which is in Jerusalem said to Honi, "I should expel you for your audacity, yet how can I, for you are Honi! God indulges you as a father does a young child who says, 'Hold me and bathe me, my father! Give to me poppy seeds and peaches and pomegranates.' And the father gives him whatsoever he may ask."

The Carob Tree

²⁹ And it came to pass that one day, Honi was traveling along a byway and came upon a man planting a carob tree. He therefore asked the man, "How long will it be before this tree bears its fruit?"

³⁰ The man told him, "Seventy years."

³¹ So Honi asked the man, "Do you think you will live

another seventy years, that you may partake of the fruit of this tree?"

³² The man said, "Perhaps I will not, But when I was born into this world, I found an abundance of carob trees that had been planted by my father and my father's father. Just as they planted trees for me, I now plant so my children and their children can partake of the fruit these trees shall bear."

³³ Then Honi sat down to have a meal, and he was overcome by sleep. And it is said that the rocks of the earth grew up around him and hid him from the eyes of the world, so that he continued to sleep for seventy years. ³⁴ When he finally awoke, he saw a man gathering fruit from the same carob tree and asked him, "Are you the man who planted this tree?"

³⁵ And the man said, "No, I am his grandson."

³⁶ Honi therefore marveled, for behold, he had slept seventy years!

³⁷ Now it was during this time that John appeared upon the earth, being a master of the waters in the desert, as Honi had been. ³⁸ And as Honi fell had fallen asleep beneath a carob tree, so now John came forth eating carob seeds with wild honey and cakes, and the roots of trees. This is a great mystery.

³⁹ Let him who has ears to hear, hear!

And let the one who dares, understand!

John's Baptism

[40] John now went out to the Jordan wearing camel's hair and the pelts of animals, girded in a belt of leather. He lived in a desolate area in which there are many caves and rocky inclines. [41] And here men came out to hear him speak, saying, "Turn from your ways, for the realm of God has come!" All manner of men came out to him, and he counseled them. [42] To the tax collectors, he said, "Do not collect any more than your due." [43] To the soldiers, he said, "Do not demand money from the people, but be content with your pay." [44] And to the multitude, he said, "The one with two tunics should share with he who has none, and your food should be shared in like manner." Whereupon he would cleanse them in the river.

[45] Now Jesus went out also with the multitude and

came to John for anointing in the waters. But recognizing him, John objected, saying, "I need to be baptized by you. Why do you come to me?"

[46] Yet Jesus knew that this was to fulfill what had been said of him, that he be born of water and the spirit, and so he humbled himself to receive John's baptism. [47] And immediately Jesus saw the spirit came upon him like a dove and heard a voice from the heavens saying, "I am well pleased with you, my son. On this day have I begotten you." [48] This was the voice of his mother in spirit, the great goddess Astarte, known to the Egyptians as Isis and the Greeks as Aphrodite. From old was she the consort of the Hebrew god, before his priesthood shunned her. [49] Her symbol is the dove of peace and the great star Sirius enclosed within a circle, the star which had appeared to the magi in heralding his first birth. Now also was it present at his second as well.

[50] And he went away from that place. And he took to himself twelve followers, one for each of the tribes in Israel and each house of his heavenly father. For he would say to them, "In my father's house are many dwellings. Were it

not so, I would not say it to you." [51] By this he meant the twelve houses in the stars, and he promised his disciples that he would go ahead of them and prepare a place for them, ascending to the heavens just as his father had done in days of yore.

[52] Yet they comprehended not the meaning of his words.

[53] His four brothers were among them, as was Matthew, a tax collector, and a man named Philip and one called Thaddaeus. [54] Some who followed him had followed John, among whom some started baptizing as he had done. But Jesus himself did not baptize. [55] And there arose a disagreement between John's disciples and certain others, because many were crossing over the Jordan to be baptized by Jesus' disciples instead. [56] And John said, "A man can only receive what is granted him in heaven. The bride belongs to the bridegroom. The bridegroom's friend attends him and listens for him, and he is joyful on hearing the bridegroom's voice."

[57] In so saying, he identified Jesus as Solomon, the bridegroom of old, and foretold the sacred wedding that was to come. [58] And Jesus himself said of John, "If you are able to accept this, he is Elijah who was to come. He who has ears to hear, let him hear."

5

¹ Simon, James and John were fishermen, and they plied their trade in the lake called Gennesaret. One day, Jesus came to the lake and saw two boats sitting there, but the fishermen were not in them but rather nearby, cleaning their nets. ² He entered into one of the boats, which was Simon's, and bade him put out a little from the land. Then he sat down and began to speak to those who were nearby, teaching them from the boat. ³ When he had finished, he

said to Simon, "Put out into the deep waters, and let down your nets for a catch."

⁴ And Simon replied, saying, "We have worked all night and taken in nothing, but at your word, I will let down the net." ⁵ And behold, they caught a great multitude. So they called out to James and John to bring their boat as well, and they worked until both vessels had been filled. ⁶ Then they went forth to the home of Simon, who was married and lived there with the mother of his wife. ⁷ This woman, however, was sick with fever. Therefore did Jesus take her by the hand, healing her in the manner of the Therapeutae so that the fever left her and she rose up and went about caring for them.

⁸ After this, they went to Capernaum, Nahum's village on the lake's northwest shore. It was a small village with a synagogue and a fertile spring, and Jesus taught there.

⁹ When he was coming to enter the town, a centurion from the Roman army came up to him and sought his help, saying, "My servant suffers greatly, for he is paralyzed."

¹⁰ Jesus said, "I will go to him."

¹¹ But the centurion told him, "I am undeserving that you should be a guest in my home. Yet if you only say the word, my servant shall be healed. ¹² For I myself am a man under authority, with soldiers who are bound to do my bidding. If I tell this one, 'Go!,' then he will go; and that one, 'Come!' and he will come. I tell my servant to do this thing, and he does it."

¹³ Jesus was astonished at the man's words and said to those around him, "Truly I say to you, I have found no one

in Israel with faith such as this.

¹⁴ "Go," he said to the centurion. And word soon
spread that the servant's condition improved in that very
hour.

¹⁵ Hearing of this, the residents of that place brought to
him many people who were sick and taken by seizures, and
he healed their afflictions after the manner of the
Therapeutae.

The Kingdom Established

¹⁶ But when it was day, he left that village and went out
to a place of desolation, and the multitudes followed him
and besought him to remain. But he refused them and went

on his way. ¹⁷ Going out, he met a tax gatherer named Levi, with whom he conversed. Upon hearing his words, Levi left everything there and followed after him. ¹⁸ He took Jesus to his house and prepared in that place a great feast in his honor, so that many people came from round about, among whom were tax gatherers and many others. ¹⁹ Some Pharisees also were among them. And these were offended, saying, "Why do you eat with tax gatherers and transgressors?"

²⁰ But Jesus said, "Those who are healthy have no need for a physician."

²¹ When therefore his brothers saw the crowds who were following him, they began urging him, saying surely he should lay claim to the throne of Israel. ²² Yet he rebuked them, saying, "My kingdom is not of this world." And they marveled, for they understood him not.

²³ And Jesus told them, "If your leaders say to you, 'Behold, the kingdom is in the sky,' then the birds of the sky will precede you. If they say to you, 'It is in the sea,' then the fish will precede you. But rather, the kingdom is within you, and it is all around you."

²⁴ They then wondered how he would restore the kingdom if it was already established. "When," they asked him, "will the kingdom come?"

²⁵ And he said to them, "It will not come by watching for it. It will be said, 'Look here!' or 'Look there!' No, but the Father's realm is spread out upon the earth, and people see it not."

6

[1] When he had anointed Jesus with water, John went away to Philip, Mary's eldest son by Herod, who sought an interpretation for a dream in which an eagle appeared and tore out both his eyes. He summoned many of his advisors and soothsayers, but none could tell him what it might mean. [2] It was then that John appeared and spoke to him directly, saying: "The dream which you have seen is of God. Now the eagle is your deceit and corruption, for it is violent and full of avarice, and this will take away your eyes, which are symbols of your dominions and your wife."

[3] John departed, but Philip's wife Herodias betrayed her

husband with his half-brother, Antipas, and went away to marry him. Then Philip's life was taken from him, whereupon his lands were forfeit to Agrippa.

⁴ But John continued to baptize in the Jordan, and he told those who came to him, "I am sent of God that you may know his laws, and that you may free yourself from those who hold power, so that no mortal may rule over you but only the Most High God."

⁵ And the rulers, hearing of this, sent men out to spy on him and trap him. ⁶ But he recognized and rebuked them, saying, "O brood of vipers! Who warned you to flee from the wrath that is to come? Turn from your ways and produce the fruit of repentance. ⁷ But do not think you can say to yourselves, 'We have Abraham as our father.' I tell you truly that God can raise from these stones children unto Abraham. ⁸Behold! The ax is at the root of the trees, and every one that does not bear good fruit will be cut down and cast into the fire."

⁹ All these things they reported back to their masters, and Antipas the tetrarch of Galilee, another of Herod's sons, grew suspicious. For the multitudes were gathering to him, and were moved by his words, and it was feared that they might start a rebellion. ¹⁰ Antipas therefore sent men to lay hands on John and remove him forcibly to the fortress called Machaerus, and there to have him imprisoned.

¹¹ About this time, Jesus was becoming known throughout the countryside for healing those who came to him. John therefore sent messengers to question him. ¹²

And Jesus said to them, "Report to your master what you have seen. The blind receive sight, the lame walk, the lepers are cleansed, the deaf hear, those who have died receive new life and good news is taken to the poor."

[13] Now he said these things to fulfill the words of the prophet, who proclaimed wonder upon wonder, declaring:

[14] In that day, the deaf will hearken
   To the words of the scroll
   And from the gloom and the darkness,
   Blind eyes shall have their sight
[15] The wayward shall gain understanding
   And those who find fault will accept instruction

[16] Many who had gone out to hear John in the wilderness were there at that time, and Jesus questioned them, saying, "What did you think you would see there in the desert? A man dressed in finery? No, for those in fine clothes are found in palaces. A prophet? And yes, more than a prophet. [17] This is he of whom it is written, 'I shall send my messenger before you, to prepare a way for you.' "

[18] Those who had been baptized by John accepted his words and followed them, and many of his followers began gathering now to Jesus. In those days, many thousands gathered to hear him speak.

[19] Now John had rebuked Antipas for his marriage to Herodias, saying he had acted unlawfully by marrying the wife of his brother while he still lived.

[20] So it came about that a feast was planned in honor of

Antipas' birthday, and when news of it reached Herodias, she arranged to have her daughter Salome dance as a gift for him. [21] When, therefore, she appeared at the celebration, her dancing so pleased the tetrarch that he offered her anything she might request of him, up to half his kingdom.

[22] Hearing this, she asked that he deliver to her John the Baptist's head upon a platter, so he sent word to Machaerus and ordered him put to death.

[23] Now there are some who say that Antipas was loath to comply with her request, but did so only because he feared what his guests might think should he fail to keep his word.

But others say that Antipas feared John's followers and sought a convenient excuse to kill him.

Return to Galilee

[24] Yet Antipas, seeing that Jesus now commanded the crowds that once had gone after John, grew once more suspicious, saying, "Is this John, now raised from the dead? Behold the powers he commands!"

[25] But Salome went away and became his disciple.

[26] And Jesus took his followers away from Judea and returned to Galilee. Among them were men and women, also: Mary who is called Magdalene or "the Tower," and Suzanna, and Joanna the wife of Cuza, who managed the household of Herod Antipas, and also Salome, the daughter of Herodias. [27] These women used their own means to support him in his travels, though his brother Judas kept charge of the money.

[28] Now first among these was Mary, his consort, who kissed him often on the mouth. [29] This offended some among them, who said to him, "Why do you love her more than the rest of us?" [30] Yet he answered and said to them, "When a blind man and one who sees are together in the darkness, they are no different from one another. But when the light comes, he who sees will see the light, but lo, he who is blind will in darkness remain."

[31] And they marveled at this, for they knew not the meaning of his words.

7

¹ It came to pass that Jesus went away into the desert, where he sojourned alone with the wild animals for forty days and forty nights. ² Now the desert lands are consecrated unto Set, the god of Egypt whose abode is the dark red wastelands. ³ It is he who is called Satan by some, the adversary who contended with Horus for the throne of heaven.

As it was written:

⁴ Osiris who is first among the Westerners
    The great god, lord of Abydos, is justified
    His son Horus reigns here
⁵ The lands of the south are in his grasp
    The lands of the north follow after him

The banks of Horus are his portion
⁶ O Set, you are expelled into the regions far afield
The great gods guard you
⁷ You shall neither come nor descend upon this kingdom
So it is, by the order of Ra's majesty

⁸ When Jesus had gone out into these regions, he began to fast and meditate, until he became hungry. ⁹ Then the spirit of Set came to him and began to beseech him, saying, "If you are the Son of God, make these stones become bread!"

¹⁰ But Jesus rebuked him, saying, "It is written that a man shall not live by bread alone, but by every word that goes forth on the breath of God." And in so saying, he declared himself man, not god, and in this way he spurned the path of hubris.

¹¹ Yet his adversary did not leave him, but instead removed him to a lofty peak whence he gazed upon the kingdoms of the world, beholding their splendor. And he said to him, "All this will I give you if you will bow and worship me."

¹² But Jesus rebuked him, saying, "Depart from me, O adversary! It is written, 'Worship the lord your god and serve him only.' " And in so saying, he declared himself a servant, not a king, and in this way he spurned the path of desire.

¹³ Yet his adversary did not leave him, but led him to the highest point of the temple, for this was the place

reserved for the phoenix. And he said to him, "Cast yourself down, for it is written: 'He will command his messengers concerning you, and they will lift you up in their hands that your foot will strike no stone.' "

[14] But Jesus rebuked him, saying, "It is likewise written: 'Do not put the lord your god to the test!' " And in so saying, he committed himself to humility and spurned the path of folly.

[15] Therefore Set did leave him, as it is written:

[16] "Your crime has been set before Ra
    The ruin you have inflicted
    Has been made known to the great god
[17] The great council confers
    And Thoth sits in judgment

[18] They report to all the grief that you have caused
    They tell of the injury you have created
    They deliver you to the devourer."

[19] And Jesus was met by messengers who cared for him until he had recovered from his sojourn.

8

¹ Now it came to pass that Jesus betook himself away from that place, saying, "The foxes have their holes, the birds of the sky have their nests, and this son of man has no place to lay his head." For he had been rejected in his own hometown and had found no rest by the Jordan, where John was baptizing.

² Behold, he said, "My condition is hunger; my inner garment is affliction and my outer garment wool. The sun is my warmth in winter, and my candle is the moon. ³My feet bear me to and fro, and the fruits of the earth do

nourish me. Neither in evening nor in morning have I any possession, yet no one on earth is richer than I."

⁴ His followers made a place for him where his beloved, Mary, lived with her sister Martha and their brother Simon, who was rich and had arranged for them to stay there. ⁵ Simon was a Pharisee, yet he had been called unclean because he was also leprous. Even so did Jesus come into his household and accept his fellowship, for which he was thankful.

⁶ This place they called Bethany, which name they chose for its many meanings. ⁷ In some ears it was Bet Annu, which means "House of the Sun" after the city of the sun in Heliopolis. In others, it was Bet Anya, which is to say "House of the Poor" after the poor who were his companions. And in still others it was Bet Aeuni, meaning "House of Dates," for the date palm was the sacred nesting place of the phoenix.

⁸ It was also called Cana, or place of reeds, after the words of the prophet: "A bruised reed he shall not break." This became a place of refuge for him.

Bride and Bridegroom

⁹ So it was that when the time was fulfilled, it was here that Jesus took Mary aside to be his wife. ¹⁰ And as her sister Martha was busy preparing for the celebration, Mary sat at Jesus' feet and listened to him. ¹¹ Martha therefore complained, saying, "Must I do all the work myself? Instruct my sister, that she may help me."

[12] But Jesus answered and said to her, "Martha, Martha, you fret and worry over many things. But one thing only is needed. Mary has chosen the better part, and it shall not be denied her."

[13] He said this to honor her as the one who would be his bride. Therefore the scripture was fulfilled which says of Ruth, "She lay at his feet until morning." And she became the wife of Boaz, the ancestor of David. So now, in like manner, was Mary betrothed to Jesus.

[14] And a great feast was planned, and the disciples of Jesus were there with him.

[15] Jesus therefore spoke to them, saying, "A king prepared a wedding banquet for his heir, sending servants forth to invite all he knew. But these refused his invitation, so he sent again for his servants and said, 'Tell them I have

prepared a great feast! I have slaughtered my oxen and fattened cattle, and all is prepared. Come now to the wedding banquet!'

¹⁶ "Yet again they did not come. One went off to tend to his business, and another to plow his field. ¹⁷ And so the king sent his servants out yet again, this time saying to them, 'The feast is prepared, but those I have invited would not come. They do not deserve to sit at my table. Go therefore to the street corners and invite to the banquet anyone you find.'"

¹⁸ This he said to teach them in the ways of wisdom. As it is written:

¹⁹ Wisdom has built her house
    She has hewn its seven pillars
²⁰ She has prepared her meat and fermented her wine
    She has also set her table
²¹ She has sent forth her maids
    And she calls from the highest point of the city
²² "Let all who are simple come in to me!"
    To those of poor judgment she proclaims:
²³ "Come! Partake of my food!
    And drink of the wine I have mixed!"

²⁴ Some, recalling these words, believed he spoke of his betrothed. So it came to pass that many would call her Sophia, which means "wisdom." ²⁵ Yet others scoffed at this, saying that the seven pillars were seven demons that had entered into her; and these also called her a sinner and

a harlot who prostituted herself with the simple-minded. For they knew not the meaning of the scriptures, and their ears were closed.

²⁶ When it came time for the feast, as they were eating, Mary was there with Jesus. ²⁷ And at the appointed time came, she brought forth an expensive jar of alabaster, filled with perfume of pure nard, and anointed his head and feet with it. She stood behind him weeping, so that her tears fell down upon his feet; and she kissed his feet and wiped them with her tears.

²⁸ In so doing, Mary performed the ancient service of the bride to her bridegroom, preparing him for the bridal chamber by anointing his head and for his burial by anointing his feet. As it was written in the scripture of King Solomon's marriage to his beloved, "You anoint my head with oil; my cup is overflowing!"

²⁹ But it came about some of those present objected, saying, "This perfume is worth a year's wages! It should have been sold, that the money might be given to the poor." ³⁰ (They said this because some of some among his followers had begun calling themselves Ebionites, which translated means "the poor," and they coveted what had been spent.)

³¹ To this Jesus replied and said, "Leave her be! She has done a beautiful thing for me. This perfume was intended to prepare me for my burial. The poor are always with you, but it is not so with me. I tell you truly that wherever these things are spoken of throughout the land, that which she has done will be recounted in her memory."

³² And he said to them, "Many stand at the door, yet he who is solitary enters the bridal chamber."

Water and Wine

³³ Now as the celebration progressed, Jesus' mother came and said to him, "There is no more wine." And she said to the servants who were there, "Do whatever he tells you."

³⁴ Nearby them stood six stone jars, which were used for ceremonial washing, able to hold twenty to thirty gallons each. So Jesus told the servants, "Go and fill these all with water." And when they returned, the vessels were completely full. ³⁵ Jesus, seeing this, instructed them, "Draw out some and take it to the master of the banquet," by whom he meant Simon, at whose home the feast was being held.

³⁶ And behold! The water was exchanged for wine.

³⁷ This he did to honor his heavenly father Osiris, who likewise is said to have performed this same wonder.

³⁸ For he told them, "The son can do nothing of himself. He can only do that which he sees the father doing. And all things which the father does, so the son shall do as well."

³⁹ And when the master of the banquet had tasted the water, he found it had been transformed into wine. ⁴⁰ He therefore took aside the bridegroom, which is to say Jesus, and complimented him, saying, "Most would serve the best wine first, holding the lesser stock in reserve so it would go unnoticed when the guests are drunk. Yet you have saved the best for now!"

⁴¹ This he said to fulfill the command of Solomon:

⁴² Go and eat your food with gladness
  And drink your wine with joy
⁴³ For this is the time that God will favor all you do
  Ever clothed in white, your head anointed with oil
  Enjoy life with your wife, whom you love

⁴⁴ So they were married in this way on the third day, and in the course of time, she bore him a child. And their daughter was named Sarah, which means Princess. Some say she was born in Egypt – for which reason she is called "the Egyptian" – and taken thence to the coast of Gaul with Mary and Joseph of Arimathea, a friend of Jesus who was among the Jewish leaders.

9

¹ After these things, Jesus took his disciples and journeyed to Galilee by way of Samaria. ² Now the people of this land were of diverse heritage, having within their veins the blood both of Israel and of foreigners. And for this cause were they looked down upon and ridiculed, so that many travelers avoided the place entirely, taking the long way around rather than passing through the heart of the countryside.

³ Jesus, however, did not aver from taking this journey. And it came about that as he traveled, he came upon a place called Jacob's well near the town of Sychar, which

was the first capital of Israel. ⁴ Nearby this place was Mount Gerazim, which the Samaritans took for their holy place, believing it was here that Abraham had offered his son Isaac as a sacrifice to their god. (The Judeans, however, rejected this and worshiped in the temple at Jerusalem.) ⁵ Jesus, being weary, sat down by the well about the sixth hour of the day, and after a time, a Samaritan woman came there to draw out water.

⁶ "Will you give me a drink?" Jesus asked her.

⁷ She then marveled, for Jews by custom did not address Samaritans. And she answered him, saying, "You are a Jew, and I a Samaritan woman. How therefore do you ask me for a drink?"

⁸ "If you should have asked me," he said, "I would have given you living water."

⁹ But she thought he meant to draw water from the well and said to him, "Sir, you have nothing to draw with, and the well is deep. Our father Jacob dug this well and drank from it himself, as did his sons and all his flocks and herds. Are you therefore greater than he, that you can bring forth water from it without aid?"

¹⁰ Jesus therefore said to her, "Everyone who drinks of this water shall thirst again, but whosoever drinks of the water I give him shall never thirst. Indeed, this water will become in him a spring of water, welling up to life eternal."

¹¹ "Sir," she said, "then give me this water so that I may thirst no more, and henceforth will no longer need to come to this place and draw water."

¹² "Then go," he told her, "and call your husband, then

return."

¹³ But she said, "I have no husband."

¹⁴ And Jesus said to her, "You have truly said that you have no husband, for you have had five husbands, and the man you have now is not your husband."

¹⁵ She was amazed and said to him, "Sir, I see well you are a prophet. Therefore tell me this: Our fathers worshiped here at this mountain, but you Jews say we must worship in Jerusalem."

¹⁶ But he said to her, "Hearken unto me now, for a time is coming when you shall reverence the father neither on this mountain nor in Jerusalem. ¹⁷ Indeed, a time is coming and now is when those who do reverence truly shall approach the father in spirit and in truth, for such are the manner of men and women the father seeks. ¹⁸ God is spirit, and they that reverence him must do so in spirit and in truth."

¹⁹ The woman therefore went from there and spread the news of it in the village, saying to the townsfolk, "This man told me everything I ever did." ²⁰ Then did the Samaritans come out to him, and they urged him to stay with them. He then stayed with them two days. ²¹ But there were those who heard of these things and scorned him for accepting their hospitality, for these men bore no good will toward the Samaritans. ²² After these things, Jesus returned to his hometown, where he began to speak in the synagogue, and many marveled at his words.

²³ Some said, "Is this not a wise man!" Yet others began to grumble, asking, "Where did he get these ideas? Is

this not the son of Mary, the brother of James and Joses and Judas and Simon? Are his sisters not also among us?"

²⁴ And they were offended.

²⁵ Jesus therefore said to them, "Only in his hometown, in his own house and among his kinfolk, is a prophet without honor."

²⁶ And he went from there to speak in the synagogues in one village and the next, drawing many people to hear his wisdom.

²⁷ During this time, he was addressing the multitudes when his mother and his brothers arrived, wishing to speak with him. But they were prevented from reaching him by the crowds. ²⁸ Therefore did someone came up to him and say, "Your mother and your brothers are here to see you." ²⁹ Yet he answered and said to them, "Who are my mother and my brothers? Behold! Whoever does the will of my father in heaven, these are my brothers and my sisters and my mother!"

³⁰ But when his enemies, heard this, they said that he was exalting himself, making himself equal to God – even though this is not what he had said. Rather, he had proclaimed that all who follow the ways of the father were the sons and daughters of heaven.

³¹ He also said plainly, "The father is greater than I."

³² Even so, they came forth to accuse him of blasphemy and picked up stones to use against him.
³³ Therefore he said to them: "Behold, is it not written in your own law, 'I have said that you are gods'? ³⁴ And if he called them gods to whom the divine word was revealed –

and the scripture cannot be annulled – why do you accuse me of blasphemy for saying I am God's son? Do not believe me unless I do what the father does!"

35 They had no answer for him, as they could not dispute with the wisdom of his words. And so, enraged, they sought to seize him, but he slipped away from their grasp. 36 He did not strike at them, but exhorted his followers, saying, "Love your enemies and pray for those who persecute you, that you may be sons of your father in heaven."

The Father and the Mother

37 Philip therefore asked him, "Show us the father!"

38 And he wondered at this, saying, "How can you ask me to show you the father? Do you not realize that I am in the father and the father is in me? 39 I love the father and do his work in every detail. As the father has loved me, so I also have loved you. 40 Whoever does not love his father and mother as I do can never be my disciple. For my mother gave me flesh, but my true mother gave me life."

41 But he warned them, saying, "He who knows the father and the mother shall be called the son of a harlot." 42 Some who heard him were vexed, saying to themselves, "Who is the mother?" and "Who is the harlot?" 43 But they dared not question him about these things, which they failed to understand. They knew not that the mother he

spoke of was the great Sophia, whose name is wisdom, the same harlot who cries out in the streets for anyone who might come into her. [44] Some among them therefore scoffed, saying his earthly mother must have been a harlot, and so this rumor began to spread and persists until this day. [45] Others began saying that Mary, his consort, was a whore as well.

[46] So he taught them concerning the nature of the one spirit, saying, "Heaven stands firm with neither post nor

column, yet it stands not on its own but through the power of the one spirit.

[47] "When an archer shoots an arrow, the arrow is seen, but not the archer. Yet the archer is there. In this way do we know the power of the one spirit to sustain the heavens and the earth, which neither crumble nor fall down. We do not see this power, yet we know it is there. [48] And once the arrow's force is spent, it falls to the ground. So it is also with heaven and earth, which would pass away were it not for the power of the one spirit.

[49] "The one spirit cannot be seen in heaven or on earth, just as the one soul cannot be seen within the body. As the soul is present throughout the body, so also the one spirit resides in all creation.

[50] "The spirit is never in only one place, nor is it bound to a single place, but resides in a realm that is beyond this world. In this realm, the spirit is in two places, the first of which is the second in time. [51] There time is an illusion, and it is always in the present moment. This realm is neither created nor made, just as the one spirit is neither created nor made.

[52] And he saw that they wished to question him, but he said, "Do not ask whether all things that exist lie within the realm of which I speak. Neither ask how a thing can be without place and beyond time. [53] Not by such questions will you know the one spirit. Such wisdom is beyond the realm of questions.

[54] "Truly, the one spirit resides within all things, abiding without end.

⁵⁵ "Among all things that reside under the heaven, some may be seen and others may not. But who has seen God? For the face of God is like the wind, which no one sees. Ever abiding, God never ceases to move throughout the earth.

⁵⁶ "The children of men can only live by dwelling in the living breath of God. From sunrise to sunset they abide there; each sight and every thought resides within the divine breath. ⁵⁷ No one knows how the wind blows; they hear it, yet see not its form. It has no color, neither blue nor yellow nor white, and no one knows whence it comes.

⁵⁸ "Whosoever is born shall also die. This is the way of things for every living creature. We are born of the wind, and as we die, the wind passes from our bodies. ⁵⁹ Do our hearts and our minds belong to us? No! But they endure because the wind allows it, and when the wind departs, their lives are at an end.

⁶⁰ "No one can see when the wind will depart, and because the children of men cannot see it, they ask, 'Where is the heavenly father?' And they wonder that they cannot see him. ⁶¹ But how can earthly eyes see your father in heaven, who is not as a man that mortal eyes may perceive him? For no one can fully know the heavenly father."

The Disciples' Vision

⁶¹ One day, his disciples came to him and said, "We have seen a great house with a large altar inside it, and twelve men who appear as priests, receiving offerings."

[62] Jesus asked them, "What are these priests like?"

And the disciples, answering, said, "They appear in this place every two weeks. Some sacrifice their own children, others their wives, to the praise one of the other. Some commit murder, and other practice a multitude of lawless deeds. [63] The men who stand at the altar invoke your name, and complete their sacrifice in the midst of their own want." Then they fell silent, for they were troubled.

[63] At length, Jesus answered them, saying, "For generations shall men plant trees without fruit, shamefully invoking my name." [64]And he offered them this interpretation: "The god of this altar is the god you serve, and you are the twelve men you have seen. The cattle you have brought to sacrifice are the many you lead astray."

And they questioned him no more.

10

¹ It came to pass that five thousand men gathered to hear Jesus on the far shore of Lake Tiberius, which is called the Sea of Galilee.

² Then their eyes became fixed all the more keenly on him, and many among them were murmuring, "Here is a prophet!" ³And they sought to take him away by force to make him their king. Yet he would not allow it, for he wanted no part of earthly kingdoms, so he withdrew by himself to a mountain.

⁴ The Pharisees, however, were vexed, thinking he purposed to start a rebellion. ⁵ They therefore followed after him, and when they had found him, inquired as to how he came to be there. ⁶ He answered and said to them:

"Even did my mother, the divine spirit, take me by a single hair on my head and bring me to the great mountain called Tabor."

[7] They knew not what he meant, that he was under the protection of his divine mother, whose name is Isis. For this teaching would he give to his disciples: "The very hairs on your head are numbered! [8] Therefore I say to you, do not fear those who can kill the body but nothing more. Are not five sparrows sold for two pennies? Yet not one of them is forgotten by God! [9] Truly I say to you, anyone who speaks a word against this son of man will be forgiven, but anyone who curses the divine spirit scorns the hand stretched forth in forgiveness."

The Way of Forgiveness

[10] He therefore taught them, "Forgive your fellows, that you may be forgiven in turn. And neglect not to forgive yourself! For just as you forgive others, so shall the One Spirit forgive you."

[11] Simon Peter asked him, "How often shall we forgive one who offends us? Seven times?"

[12] But Jesus said, "I say not seven only, but seventy times seven!"

[13] It therefore began to be said among some men that, through forgiveness, he was inviting further transgression. [14] Yet did he not also say, "Do not cast your pearls before the swine"? And did he not also upbraid the Pharisees for their continual abuse?

¹⁵ He therefore spoke to them more fully of forgiveness, asking them, "Suppose one of you has a hundred sheep and loses one. Does he not therefore leave behind the ninety-nine in the open country and search for the sheep that was lost until he finds it? ¹⁶ And when he does, he puts it on his shoulders and returns home with it, calling his friends and neighbors to him and saying, 'Rejoice with me, for I have found my lost sheep.' ¹⁷ Truly I say to you, there is more joy in heaven over one who seeks forgiveness than over ninety-nine who say that they are righteous.

¹⁸ "Or suppose also that a woman has ten silver coins, yet loses one of them. Does she not light a lamp and sweep the house, searching carefully until she finds it? And when she does, she tells her friends and neighbors to come and rejoice with her that she has found the coin she had lost.

¹⁹ "Now a certain man had two sons. And the younger went to his father, saying, 'Give to me my share of the estate.' So the man divided his property between the two of them.

²⁰ "Not long afterward, the younger son gathered up all his belongings and set off on a journey to a distant land, and once there he squandered all his wealth on lavish, carefree living. ²¹ Then a severe famine came upon the land, and he began to be in need. So he went forth and hired himself out to a citizen of that country, who sent him into the fields to feed his pigs. ²² He longed to fill his stomach with the pods he gave over to the pigs to eat, but he received nothing from anyone.

²³ "In due course, then, he remembered his father's house, saying to himself, 'How many of my father's servants have food to spare, while here I sit starving? Therefore shall I set forth and return to my father and humble myself before him, for I have transgressed against him and against heaven. ²⁴ I shall tell him I am no longer worthy to wear his name, and I shall ask of him that he hire me as his servant.' " ²⁵ Therefore did he arise and return to the land of his father.

²⁶ "But while he was still a long ways off, his father caught sight of him on the road and was filled with compassion. Running to him, he threw his arms around his son and kissed him.

²⁷ "And his son said to him, as he had determined, 'Father, I have transgressed against heaven and against you. I am no longer fit to be called your son.'

²⁸ "But the father sent word to his servants, commanding them to be quick and bring the best robe to adorn his son who had returned. ²⁹ 'Put a ring on his finger and sandals on his feet!' he declared. 'Bring the fatted calf and kill it for a feast that we might celebrate. For this son of mine who was dead lives again, and he who was lost is now found!'

³⁰ "And they began to celebrate. ³¹ But soon it happened that the man's elder son, who was out in the field, returned to the house. And when he came near, he heard the sound of music and dancing. ³² He therefore called one of the servants to ask what had happened, and the man told him, 'Your brother has come, and your father has slain the fatted calf to celebrate his safe return.'

³³ "But the elder brother was indignant and refused to go any further, so his father came forth and besought him to come in.

³⁴ Then he answered, saying to his father, 'All these years have I slaved for you, never once refusing your commands. Yet never have you given me so much as a young goat to celebrate with my friends. Yet this son of yours has squandered your wealth with harlots and now returns home, that you may kill the fatted calf in his honor.'

³⁵ "His father therefore said to him, My son, you were ever with me, and all I have is yours. But it was only right to celebrate and be joyful, for this brother of yours was dead and is now alive again. He was lost and has been found!"

The Sign of Jonah

³⁶ But the Pharisees heeded not his words and knew not their meaning. They looked only on the outside of the dish, neglecting to search inside. ³⁷ Loving the law, they shunned the spirit. Holding to the way of judgment, they knew not the way of love. ³⁸ Caring not for his message, they sought only to see him work miracles. Therefore did they challenge him, saying: "What wonder will you perform for us that we may see it and believe in you? Our fathers ate manna in the desert, as it is written: 'He gave them bread from heaven to eat.'"

³⁹ But he chastened them, saying, "This wicked unfaithful generation asks for a sign, but none will be given except the sign of the prophet Jonah!"

⁴⁰ Then they were speechless, for they knew not the sign of which he spoke, which is the sign of renewal from

the depths of despair. For they sought not renewal but an excuse to pass judgment upon him.

⁴¹ He therefore performed no wonder for them to see.

⁴² After these things, his disciples came to him and started to ask him about the kingdom of heaven, so he began speaking to them in stories and parables.

⁴³ They asked him, "Why do you speak to us in this way?"

⁴⁴ And he said, "To you have the secrets of the kingdom been imparted, but not to these others. For though seeing, they see not, and though hearing, the do not listen or understand. ⁴⁵ In them is fulfilled the word of Isaiah:

⁴⁶ You shall be ever hearing, but never knowing
    You shall be ever seeing, yet not perceiving
⁴⁷ For this people's hearts have become calloused
    ⁴⁸ They scarcely hear with their ears
    And have closed their eyes
⁴⁹ Otherwise, they might see with their eyes,
    And hear with their ears
    And understand in their hearts
    And turn, and I would heal them.

⁵⁰ "Yet blessed are your eyes because they see, and your ears because they hear." ⁵¹ (These were the teachings of the Therapeutae, who brought forth the ways of their ancestors by way of allegory and parable, believing that words were but symbols that concealed deeper secrets.)

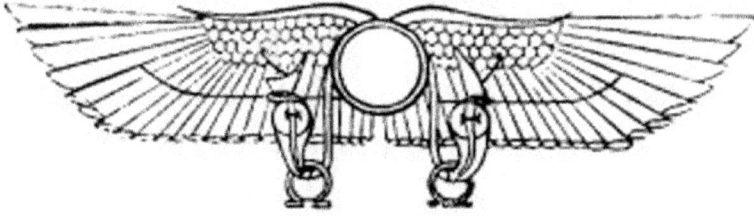

The Realm of Heaven

[52] And Jesus told them many things about the realm of God, saying, "It is like a mustard seed, which a man took and planted in his field. [53] Although it is the smallest of all seeds, when it grows it becomes the largest of garden plants, as large as a tree, so that the birds of the air come and perch among its branches."

[54] And he said also, "The realm of heaven is like yeast, which a woman took and mixed into a large amount of flour until it worked all through the dough."

[55] And again, "The realm of heaven is like a woman carrying a jar full of meal. And while she traveled a distant road, the handle of the jar broke and meal began to spill out behind her on the road. [56] Yet she was unaware, not knowing her misfortune, until she returned to her own home and opened the jar to find it empty."

[57] And he told them still another parable: "The realm of the father is like a woman who took a little leaven and hid it within the dough and, working it through, made from it large loaves."

[58] Then he said to them, "The realm of heaven is like a

treasure buried in a field. [59] Now a certain man discovered it, and he hid it once more, then in his joy went and sold all he had to buy that field. [60] And it is like a merchant who went looking for fine pearls: When he found one of great value, he went and sold everything he had to purchase it.

[61] "To you I give the keys to this realm. And whatsoever you bind on earth will be bound in heaven; and whatsoever you loose on earth will be loosed in heaven. For this realm is fashioned after a realm imperishable."

[62] These things too were the teachings of the Eygptian magi, who had a saying, "As above, so below."

11

¹ Jesus' disciples therefore asked him, "What existed before heaven and earth came into being?"

² And he told them, "There was darkness and water, and spirit upon the water. And truly I say to you, what you seek and ask after, behold, it is within you."

³ They marveled at his words, that something within them should have existed before earth and even heaven.

⁴ And they saw a baby nursing at his mother's breast nearby.

⁵ And Jesus said, "Truly I say to you, unless you change and become like little children, you will never enter the kingdom. ⁶ Therefore, whoever humbles himself like this

child is the greatest in the kingdom of heaven."

7 They asked him, therefore, "Are we to enter the kingdom as infants?"

8 And he said to them, "When you make the two become one, and the inner like the outer, and the outer like the inner, you will you enter. 9 When you make the upper like the lower, and the male and female into a single one, so that they are neither male nor female, then shall you enter.

10 "All nature, and everything there is, and every earthly creature – all these exist in and with one another. For the nature of earthly things is to dissolve into the root of their own being. He who has ears to hear, let him hear."

11 They wondered at these things, not understanding that he spoke of the cycle of birth, death and renewal that was manifest each day all about them. As the wise king Solomon has said:

12 Generations rise and fall
    But the earth endures forever
13 The sun rises up and sets again
    Then hurries back to where it rises
14 The wind blows to the south
    Then turns to the north
15 Round and round it goes,
    Ever returning to its course

16 All streams flow to the sea
    Yet the seas are never full
17 For the place streams come from,

To this place do they ever return
¹⁸ The eye will never have its fill of seeing
Nor the ear its fill of hearing
¹⁹ All that has been done will be done once again
For there is nothing new under the sun

²⁰ Then they asked him, "When shall we rest, and when will the kingdom come?"

²¹ And he said, "What you look forward to is here already, yet you do not see it."

²² So then they asked him, "How will our end be?"

²³ But he admonished them, saying, "Have you already discovered the beginning, that you seek now for the end? Where the beginning is, there the end shall be! Blessed is he who takes his place in the beginning, for such a one shall know the end and will not face death."

²⁴ When he saw they did not comprehend his words, Jesus therefore spoke to them in plain terms.

Who Do You Say I Am?

²⁵ And he asked them, "Who do people say that I am?"

²⁶ They replied, "Some say you are Elijah. Others that you are John, the baptizer. Still others say that you are Jeremiah or one of the prophets." ²⁷ (Now by this they testified to the hope of taking on new flesh once their body was committed to the grave, for Jesus himself had said to them that John was Elijah in new flesh.)

²⁷ Jesus then told them, "The names that are given to

worldly things are the cause of great deception. For they turn men's hearts from what is true to an illusion. The names which are heard belong to this world."

²⁸ And he told them a parable: "Some rulers wanted to deceive a man, for they saw that he was virtuous. So he took the name 'good' and ascribed it to that which would not profit him. ²⁹ In doing so, they sought to deceive him by binding a name to that which was not good. ³⁰ And then, as though doing him a favor, they invited him to forsake that which was good by calling it 'not good.' For they wished to take the free man and make him their slave forever."

³¹ He therefore admonished them, saying, "You have heard that it was said in days of old, 'Do not break an oath.' But I tell you to make no oath at all, either by heaven which is the throne of God or by earth which is his footstool. ³² And do not swear by your head, for you cannot make one hair of it white or black. But simply let your yes be yes and your no be no."

³³ He spoke these things so that they might understand the power of the word to tear down, as well as to build up. For he said, "Truth did not enter the world naked, but came adorned in forms and images. Otherwise, the world could not perceive it."

³⁴ Having said these things, he asked them again, "Now, who do you say I am?"

³⁵ And one among them said to him, "Truly, you are the messiah, the son of the living God."

³⁶ But he urged them not to speak thus.

The Way of Humility

[37] And yet his brothers pressed him, saying, "No one who wants to become a public figure acts in secret. Therefore, show yourself to the world!"

[38] He therefore spoke to them of the Pharisees and teachers of the law. [39] "All they do is done for men to see! They make their phylacteries wide and adorn their robes with long tassels. They pride themselves in taking the place of honor at a banquet or the most important seats in the synagogue, and they love to be greeted as 'Rabbi' in the town market.

[40] "But I say to you, do not be called 'Rabbi,' for you

have only one teacher, who is your father in heaven, and all of you are brothers. [41] I tell you plainly: Whoever exalts himself will be humbled, but the one who humbles himself is raised up.

[42] "The greatest among you should be as the youngest, and the one who rules like the one who serves. [43] I ask you, who is greater? Is it the one seated at the table or the one who serves him? Is it not the one at the table? But I am among you as one who serves." [44] (In so saying, he exalted the tradition of the Therapeutae, who are called servants).

[45] And he instructed them, "Take heed that you do not perform acts of virtue to be seen by men, for if you do, you will have no reward from your heavenly father. [46] Therefore when you give to the needy, do not announce it with great fanfare to be praised by men, as the hypocrites do in the streets and the synagogues. [47] But instead, do not let your left hand know what your right hand is doing, that your giving may be done in secret. Then your father, who sees the secret things, will reward you."

[48] When men would praise him, therefore, he would withdraw from them. And when they sought to exalt him, he practiced humility. [49] It therefore came about that some of his followers sought to take him by force and make him their king. But he, knowing their hearts, removed himself from their presence and went away by himself to a mountain.

[50] He would go off early in the morning, seeking out lonely places in which to pray, telling his disciples: "When you pray, to not be like the hypocrites who love to stand

and pray in the synagogues and on street corners to be seen by men. Truly I say, they have received their entire reward. [51] But when you pray, go to your room and close the door, and there pray to your father, who is unseen. Then he who sees what is done in secret shall reward you."

[52] Likewise, when he healed men of their afflictions, he would instruct them to tell no one.

[53] On a certain day, a man afflicted with leprosy came to him and pleaded with him for help, saying, "Master, if you are willing, you can make me clean."

[54] Jesus therefore reached out and touched the man, saying, "I am willing. Be clean," whereupon the leprosy departed from him.

[55] In so doing, he announced an end to the ancient laws of uncleanness, which have in every age divided the sons of men. And he proclaimed a new age, wherein the walls of division would be torn down and the veils obscuring truth would be rent asunder.

12

¹ Now the Sabbath, which is the day of rest, had arrived. And Jesus was passing through some grain fields on that day. ² His disciples had grown hungry and began to pick some heads of grain to eat them. ³ When some Pharisees who were nearby witnessed this, they became alarmed and accused him, saying, "Behold! Your disciples do that which is unlawful in profaning the Sabbath!"

⁴ But Jesus said to them, "Have you not read what David did when he and his fellows were hungry? He entered the House of God, and they partook of the bread

that had been consecrated, which was not intended for them but only for the priests. ⁵ Or have you not read in the law that the temple priests are innocent, though they desecrate the Sabbath? ⁶ Had you known the meaning of these words, 'I desire mercy, not sacrifice,' you would not have condemned the innocent. A son of man is lord of the Sabbath."

⁷ Then they asked him also, "Why do your disciples despise the traditions of the elders, for they do not wash their hands before eating?"

⁸ Yet Jesus replied in kind: "And why do you violate God's command for the sake of your tradition? ⁹ For God said 'Honor your father and mother' and 'Anyone who curses his father or mother must be put to death.' ¹⁰ But you counsel a man to withhold blessings from his mother and father, telling them, 'Whatever help you might otherwise have received from me is a gift devoted to God!' In so doing you nullify the word of God for the sake of your tradition. ¹¹ You hypocrites! Isaiah spoke truly when he prophesied about you:

> These people honor me with their lips
>> But their hearts are far from me
> ¹² They worship me in vain
>> Their teachings are nothing more
>> than rules devised by men

¹³ Now a crowd had gathered, and Jesus spoke to them, saying, "Hear and understand. What enters a man's mouth

does not make him unclean, but that which proceeds from his mouth defiles him."

¹⁴ Afterward his disciples came to him and said, "Do you know that the Pharisees were offended by your words?"

¹⁵ But he said, "Leave them. They are blind guides. If a blind man leads a blind man, they shall both fall into a pit."

¹⁶ Jesus then went from that place to a synagogue and beheld a man whose hand was shriveled. And his enemies, looking for cause to impeach him, went to ask him: "Is it lawful to heal on the Sabbath?"

¹⁷ So he asked them, "If any of you has a sheep that falls into a pit on the Sabbath, will you not lay hold of it and raise it up? And what value has a sheep and what value has a man? Therefore I say to you that it is lawful to do good on the Sabbath!"

Teachings of Jesus

¹⁸ These are the teachings of Jesus.

¹⁹ "Do not judge, lest you yourselves incur judgment. For as you judge others, so shall you be judged in like manner, and the measure you use shall be used to measure you.

²⁰ "Why do you look at the speck of sawdust in your brother's eye, yet heed not the log in your own? How can you say to your brother, 'Come, let me remove the speck from your eye,' when all the time is a log in your own? ²¹ You hypocrite! First remove the log from your own eye.

Only then can you see clearly to take the speck from the eye of your brother. [22] Know what is before your face, and that which is hidden will be disclosed to you, for nothing is hidden that will not be revealed, and nothing is buried that will not be raised."

[23] Now without judgment, there is no vengeance. He therefore counseled them also against vengeance, saying, "You have heard it was said, 'Eye for eye and tooth for tooth.' But I tell you, resist not the evil one. [24] If someone strikes you on the right cheek, turn to him the left as well. And if someone wants to sue and take your tunic, offer him also your cloak. [25] If someone forces you to go a mile with him, accompany him for two. [26] Give to the one who asks of you, and turn not away from the one who seeks to borrow.

[27] "To whoever has, more shall be given. From the one who has not, even what he thinks he has shall be removed.

[28] "You have heard it said, 'Love your neighbor and hate your enemy.' But I tell you: Love your enemies and pray for those who persecute you, that you may be sons of your father in heaven.' (In so saying, he reminded them that a son of God is not a man born of a miracle, but one who is born again from his own humility). [29] For God, he told them, "causes the sun to rise on the evil as well as the good, and he sends forth rain upon men of honor and dishonor. [30] If, therefore, you love those who love you, what honor do you deserve? Even tax collectors do as much."

[31] For this reason, he warned them against abiding in

anger, saying, "The one who curses, becomes angry or finds weakness in himself, yet does not remove it, remains far from perfection." ³² And he taught them, "Behold, you have heard it said from ages past, 'Do not murder, for a murderer brings judgment upon himself.' But I say to you that anyone who is angry with his brother incurs judgment."

³³ These things he said knowing that the thoughts of a man are made manifest in action.

³⁴ They wanted to know from him the essence of all things, so he shared with them four principles.

³⁵ The first is this: Begin by freeing yourself from all desire, for if the heart is set on something, it gives rise to every sort falsehood. And false thinking gives rise to false action.

³⁶ The second is this: Be still. Wear no mask and make no pretense to being what you are not.

³⁷ The third is this: Do not trumpet your good deeds for people to hear. Do what is right and hold to the truth, but not to make a name for yourself. Practice the way of light to bring life to the truth; then you will know peace and joy.

³⁸ The fourth is this: Seek not to control your life. Do not take sides in disputes concerning good and evil, but accept all people equally and live from day to day. A clear glass reflects all things, in every color and down to the smallest detail. Be as a glass and reflect without judgment.

³⁹ Someone asked him, "What is the greatest commandment?"

[40] And he answered, "Love the lord your God with all your heart, soul and mind. This is the first and foremost commandment. And the second is like it: Love your neighbor as yourself. All the law and the prophets are based upon these two commandments." [41] He charged them: "Be not content, save when you regard your brother with love. [42] This is my command, that you love one another. Love your brother like your soul, guard him like the pupil of your eye. In everything do to others as you would have them do to you."

[43] This had also been the teaching of Ma'at in Egypt, and the great rabbi Hillel had counseled his disciples, "That which is hateful to you, do not do to your fellow. That is the whole of the Torah. The rest is explanation. Go and learn."

[44] Jesus therefore told them, "With respect to all living creatures, always act in kindness and refrain from cruel thoughts. The one who does this shall find less cause for regret. The children of men should always do what is right toward all living things.

[45] "Faith receives and love gives. No one can receive without faith, so also no one can give without love. And if anyone gives without love, he has no benefit from what he has given."

[46] And some were perplexed, murmuring, "What then of the law?"

[47] But he said, "Do not presume that I have come to abolish the law or the prophets; I have come not to abolish, but to perfect them! [48] I tell you truly, until heaven and

earth pass away, not the smallest letter or the least stroke of a pen will disappear from the law until all things are accomplished! [49] Anyone who breaks the least commandments and teaches others to do the same will be called least in the realm of heaven, yet whosoever practices and teaches these commands will be called great in the realm of heaven!

[50] "Truly I say to you, unless your virtue exceeds that of the scribes and Pharisees, you will surely not enter the realm of heaven."

Women Exalted

[51] He therefore taught them: "You have heard it said, 'Do not lie with another man's wife.' But I tell you that anyone who looks at a woman with desire has already lain with her in his heart. [52] And it has also been said, 'The man who divorces his wife must give her a certificate of divorce. But I tell you that any man who divorces his wife, except if she be unfaithful, causes her to commit adultery. And the man who marries a divorced woman commits adultery in like manner.'

[53] He said these things because it had become the habit of men to send their wives away upon a whim, each that he might marry another. [54] In so doing, it was said, they brought shame upon the ones rejected. Yet in truth, through their folly, they brought shame upon themselves.

[55] Some among his companions found these sayings

hard to accept. These spoke out against the women who were among them, rebuking Jesus for the sake of his consort, Mary. [56] One day, Simon Peter rebuked him, "Let Mary leave us, for women are not worthy of this life." But Jesus resisted him. [57] So Simon took the others aside, saying, "Has he really spoken privately with a woman and not openly with us? Did he prefer her over us, and are we to therefore hearken to her?"

[58] Mary therefore wept when she heard this.

[59] And another among them disputed with Simon, saying, "You have always been quick to anger, and now you are contending against this woman as though she were an adversary. [60] But if the master made her worthy, who are you to reject her? Surely he knows her well, and this is why

he has loved her more than us."

⁶¹ For this reason, she was called an apostle.

⁶² And in this same way did Jesus give honor to all women.

Teachings of the Disciples

⁶³ As Jesus shared wisdom with his followers, they in turn shared what was received of him.

⁶⁴ These, therefore, are their teachings:

⁶⁵ They spoke of wisdom: "If any of you should lack wisdom, let him ask of God, who gives to all generously and without reproach. And it shall be given to him."

⁶⁶ And then, that all things are connected: "For the body has not one part, but many. And if the foot should protest, 'I am not a hand, therefore I am not of the body,' this would in no way make it so. And if the ear should say, 'Since I am not an eye, I am not of the body,' it would not for this reason belong to the body any less. ⁶⁷ If all the body were an eye, where would hearing be? And if all the body were an ear, how could there be smell?

⁶⁸ "So there are many parts, but one body. The eye cannot dismiss the hand, saying it is not needed. Neither can the head declare that it does not need the feet. ⁶⁹ On the contrary, those parts which seem weaker are indispensable, and the parts that seem to us less honorable are treated with great honor. ⁷⁰ If one part suffers, all others suffer with it, and if one is honored, all the others likewise rejoice."

71 And again, on the excellence of love: "Love one another, for love is of God. They that love are born of God and know God. They that do not love know not God, for God is love."

72 "If I speak in the tongues of men and angels, yet have not love, I am a naught but a resounding gong or a clanging cymbal. 73 If I prophesy and understand all mysteries and knowledge, and I have faith that moves a mountain, yet I have not love, I am nothing. 74 If I give all my goods to help the poor and surrender my body to flames, but have not love, it profits me not at all.

75 "Love is patient. Love is kind. It is not given to envy and does not boast. It is not prideful, rude or self-seeking. It is slow to anger and keeps no account of wrongs suffered. 76 Love delights not in cruelty but rejoices in truth. It ever protects, ever trusts, ever hopes and perseveres always.

77 "Love never fails."

13

¹ In those days, it came to pass that Jesus received word from Bethany that Simon the Pharisee, the brother of Mary and Martha, was sick. ² This was the rich man who had been afflicted with leprosy, at whose home Jesus had stayed. And Mary had gone home to minster to him.

³ Messengers therefore came to him on the road with this news, but Jesus plainly told them, "This illness will not end in death," and he tarried two more days before he

arrived, making ready for the task that lay ahead of him. [4] This was the great mystery of the heavenly father Osiris, whose name was Al Asar or Eleazar, which in the Greek is Lazarus.

[5] From days of old, the Egyptian priests had raised up and purified the fallen king from among the sleeping in the great necropolis at Heliopolis, declaring, "I have come for you that I might clean you, cleanse you and revive you. Rise up and live!"

[6] So now Jesus set about to raise and purify Simon from his afflictions. Therefore was he set in a tomb for four days and given the name Lazarus after the manner of the heavenly father who had risen up before him, that he might partake in his mystery. [7] As it was written, "Horus dispels the evil that was upon you for four days."

[8] At the end of these four days, Jesus went forth to him in the manner of Horus.

[9] When she heard Jesus was coming, Mary stayed behind, but Martha came out to meet him on the road, reproaching him for the delay. But he told her, "Your brother will rise again."

[10] At length he came to the place where they were, in Bethany, where a great crowd had gathered, for Simon was both rich and influential. [11] The Pharisees had gathered there as well, for Simon himself was a Pharisee, but a great many of those who had come out to him were enemies of Jesus who had come to spy on him and report to the ruling council, called the Sanhedrin.

[12] When she saw Jesus coming, Mary came out weeping

and lamenting over her brother, so that Jesus was deeply moved in spirit and troubled. He therefore asked her, "Where have you laid him?"

¹³ She said, "Come. Behold."

¹⁴ Jesus wept.

The Raising of Lazarus

¹⁵ Simon had been laid within a cave and wrapped in burial cloths, as was the custom through all the ages, and a rock have been placed across the entryway. ¹⁶ These things were done in homage to the earth, who takes the fallen again to her bosom and brings forth new life from the darkness of her womb. As Jesus had said, "You must be born anew." ¹⁷ Now was Simon's time to be born anew and be cleansed of the leprosy with which he was afflicted.

¹⁸ Then did those standing by remove the stone from the mouth of the cave, releasing the stench of his sickness.

¹⁹ And Jesus proclaimed, "Lazarus, come forth!"

²⁰ In this moment, Simon came out to them, still wrapped in the burial garments they had placed on him, a cloth set over his face and his hands bound in strips of linen. ²¹ And Jesus said, "Remove these garments and let him go!"

²² Now the Pharisees who had come to spy on Jesus went back to those who had sent them and reported everything they had seen. And their reports reached the ears of the chief priests, whereupon they called a meeting of the Sanhedrin to discuss these matters.

[23] "What are we accomplishing?" they asked. "Here this man is performing deeds of wonder. If we allow him to continue, all the people will flock to him and the Romans will come to take away our both our temple and our nation."

[24] They said this because Caesar had entrusted them with keeping the peace, and they feared losing their positions of influence on the council. But they were loath to lay their hands on him because they feared the crowds he commanded.

[25] Yet one named Caiaphas, who was the high priest at that time, silenced them, saying, "You know nothing at all! Do you not understand that it is better for you that one man die for the people than that the entire nation perish?"

[26] So they resolved then and there to kill him.

14

¹ After these things, Jesus decided to travel to Jerusalem for the Passover feast, so he began making his way toward the city.

² And he came to Jericho, that ancient city near the west bank of the Jordan, and there found a wealthy tax collector named Zacchaeus who had climbed a sycamore tree in order to see him above the crowds. ³ Catching sight of this man, Jesus said, "Come down at once, for I must stay at your home this night."

⁴ Zacchaeus therefore came down from where he had been watching and welcomed him. But some who were

nearby were grumbling, because Jesus was to stay at the home of a tax gatherer.

⁵ But Zacchaeus stood up and declared to all within hearing, "This very day I give half my possessions to the poor. And to any man who I have cheated, I shall repay that one four times!"

⁶ Jesus replied, "Vindication has come to this house today!"

⁷ After these things, he sent two of his disciples ahead of him to a village near the Mount of Olives, which is just outside the city, and told them, "Go into that village, and there you shall find a colt tied up by the entrance to the place. Untie it and bring it to me. ⁸ And if anyone asks you what you are about, tell them that I need it and will return it shortly."

⁹ And they followed his instructions, finding everything as he had said. ¹⁰ Seeing a donkey's colt outside in the street, secured to a doorway, they went to untie it. Some people nearby asked them what they were doing, but when they told them Jesus had need of it, they let them continue about their business.

¹¹ They therefore returned the colt to Jesus and tossed their cloaks over its back so he could ride it, for the donkey was an animal of Set. ¹² In this way, he set an example for humility by following in the way of the seer and sorcerer Balaam, who in the same manner rode on the back of a donkey to bless the nation of Israel. ¹³ If anyone can accept this, Balaam was a forerunner of Jesus. He had said before him, "I cannot do anything of my own accord, for good or

ill, that goes beyond the command of the Lord. And I must say only what the Lord says." [14] In like manner had Jesus declared, "The words I speak to you are not my own, but they are the words of the father who speaks from within me."

[15] But Balaam, when he set forth on his journey, had been waylaid by a messenger from the god of Israel, who stood in the midst of the road so that his ass could go no further. [16] And in his anger, he beat the animal that had been faithful to him many years, so that she cried out to him, protesting this treatment.

[17] Yet the ass Jesus rode neither strayed from its course nor cried out, continuing onward toward Jerusalem.

[18] Him who has ears to hear, let him hear.

The Humble Entry

[19] And men came forth and laid their cloaks before him on the road and spread branches they had cut in the fields,

for they wished to proclaim him their king, shouting, "Hosanna! Blessed is he who comes in the name of the lord! Blessed be the coming kingdom of our father David! Hosanna in the highest!"

20 But again they had not understood him. For he had said: "He who has become rich, let that one be a king. But let he who has power renounce it! He who knows everything but fails to know himself misses everything!"

21 Yet not perceiving his humility as an example to be followed, they instead sought to lift him up. 22 He therefore tarried not long inside the city, but departed from that place and returned with his companions to Bethany. 23 And his anger burned within him, for no man had understood his message. The blessing he might have brought into the city instead became a curse.

24 When, therefore, he went forth again the next morning and saw a barren fig tree standing by the road (for it was not the season for figs), he laid his curse upon it, saying, "May you never again bear fruit!"

25 For just as his teachings had failed to bear fruit among the people, so had the fig tree failed to bear its fruit.

26 But his disciples saw him do this, and it brought to mind a parable he had shared with them:

27 A farmer went out to sow some seed. 28 Some of it fell along the byways, and the birds of the air descended to eat it. 29 Some also fell upon the rocky soil, and it sprang up at once but withered just as quickly for it had no place to take root. 30 Other seed still fell among the thorns, which choked out the newly planted crops, preventing them from

yielding any grain. [31] Only a portion of the seed fell on fertile soil, whence it sprang up and produced a crop a hundred times greater than what the man had planted.

[32] So now had this seed fallen among the thorns of men who had no ears to hear and whose minds were closed to wisdom.

15

¹ The Passover feast was near at hand, and Jesus looked down upon the city and wept, saying, "Jerusalem, Jerusalem! If only you had known this day what would bring you peace ... yet now, it is hidden from your eyes!"

² When he came again into the city, he went straightway to the temple and began to confront the men who had corrupted it. ³ In this place were merchants selling sheep and doves and cattle to be sacrificed, and also money changers who made their living exchanging Greek and Roman coins for Jewish money, which alone was accepted

in the temple courts.

⁴ So making a whip of cords, Jesus began to flail it about, driving out the merchants and overturning the tables of the money changers, railing against them. ⁵ "It is written," he declared, "that my father's house will be a house of prayer. Yet you have transformed it into a den of thieves!"

⁶ Jesus watched as the wealthy came and put their gifts into the temple treasury, and presently he saw also a poor widow approach carrying two small copper coins called lepta. ⁷ And he told those standing by there, "Truly I say to you, this poor widow has given more than all the others. Everyone else gave gifts out of their abundance, but she in her want gave all she had to live on."

⁸ And he visited a dye works owned by a man named Levi, where he took seventy-two cloths of varied colors and put them in the vat. But when he removed them, all were white as snow. And he said, "Even so is this son of man come as a dyer."

⁹ Now there were seventy-two members of the Sanhedrin in Jerusalem, and these men were tainted by corruption of every sort.

¹⁰ The high men on the council were afraid at his actions in purifying the seventy-two cloths, because they thought he meant to remove them and install his disciples in their place. ¹¹ For he had appointed seventy-two of his own followers and sent them out ahead of them in pairs to seek out those who would receive his message. ¹² He had told them, "I am sending you out like sheep amongst the

wolves. Take no bag or sandals, and greet no one on the road. [13] When you enter a house, say, 'Peace be upon this house.' And if a man of peace is there, he will receive your blessing. Stay in this house and partake of all that is set before you, but do not move from house to house."

[14] He said this because he knew the dangers of sending them forth, for the authorities even then had been convinced that they planned to start a rebellion.

[15] After this, he began to teach the people of the city about the realm of God.

A Blind Man Healed

[16] Now near the Sheep Gate of the city lay a pool called Bethesda, around which there were five porches. And upon these were gathered the blind and the lame and the infirm, for it was said that at certain times a divine messenger went down into the pool and stirred up the waters. [17] And they believed that whoever was the first to step into the waters would be made whole of whatever afflicted him.

[18] A certain man lay there who had been sick for thirty-eight years. And when Jesus saw him there, he asked him, "Do you wish to be whole?"

[19] The man answered him, "There is no one to put me into the pool when the waters are stirred, so while I approach, someone always arrives before me."

[20] Jesus told him, "Arise, take up your mat and walk."

[21] And the man did so.

[22] But his enemies were moved to anger, for he had

done this on the Sabbath. Yet he told them, "My father is still working, therefore I also work."

²³ As he passed along there, he came upon a certain man who had been blind from birth. His disciples therefore asked him, "Rabbi, who has sinned, this man or his parents, that he should have been born blind?"

²⁴ Jesus said to them, "Neither has this man nor his parents sinned." ²⁵ In this way did he rebuke them for their error, for where they might have shown mercy, they sought instead to cast blame. For blame is the handmaiden of judgment, and these together beget conceit.

²⁶ So it is that conceited men have perverted the truth, calling forth judgment on all men for the evils they themselves have inflicted. Such men say that all are vile and

wretched creatures, incapable of virtue because of Adam's error. [27] Yet they know not what they say. Have they not read where it is written, "Men shall not be slain for the crimes of their fathers, nor fathers for the crimes of their sons. Nay, each man shall answer for his own crimes"? [28] And do they not know that man was created in the image of God? So therefore if man is called evil, what may be said of God?

[29] Jesus therefore told his disciples, "We have come here that the work of God may be displayed in this man's life."

[30] Then he spat on the earth, making some mud out of the spittle. And this he put into the blind man's eyes, saying, "Go now, wash in the Pool of Siloam." [31] Therefore did the man go forth as Jesus bade him, and when he went home again, his sight was restored.

[32] Some of his neighbors, seeing this, began saying to themselves, "Isn't this the same man who used to beg by the side of the road?" Yet others said no, that he only resembled him.

[33] But the man himself insisted, saying, "I am he!"

[34] "How then have your eyes been opened?" they asked him. So he told them what Jesus had done.

[35] Therefore did these men take him before the Pharisees, who asked him the same questions. And he told them, "The man Jesus put mud on my eyes, and I washed, so now I see!"

[36] But some of the Pharisees said to him, "This man is not from God, for he does not keep the Sabbath. Tell us,

what do you have to say about him?"

³⁷ The man replied, "He is a prophet."

³⁸ They took the man then to his parents and asked them about it. But they said, "This is our son, and he was born without sight. Yet as to how he now sees, we do not know. He is of age and can speak for himself." ²⁵ They said this because the leaders of the synagogue had said that any follower of Jesus would be removed from the fellowship.

³⁹ So the Pharisees told the man, "Give glory to God. As for this man, we know he is a sinner."

⁴⁰ "Whether he is a sinner or not, I do not know," said the man. "I do know that I was blind, yet now I see."

⁴¹ They pressed him, saying again to him, "What did he do to you? How did he open up your eyes?"

⁴² But the man answered, "I have told you this already, and do you now want to hear it again? Do you wish also to become his disciple?"

⁴³ So they heaped scorn upon him, saying, "It is you who are his disciple. We are disciples of Moses! We know that God spoke to Moses, but as to this one, we do not even know whence he came."

⁴⁴ The man said, "This is a wonder of wonders! You know not whence he came, yet he opened my eyes. We know God does not hearken to sinners, but he listens to the godly man who does his will. ⁴⁵ The eyes of a man born blind have been opened, a thing that has never been heard of before in Israel. If this man were not from God, he could do nothing."

⁴⁶ "You were steeped in sin at birth!" they said, casting

judgment against him for his infirmity. "How dare you lecture us!"

⁴⁷ And they cast him out.

16

¹After this, they found Jesus and confronted him about the man. Jesus therefore said to them, "For this have I come into the world, that the blind may see and those who see may become blind."

² The Pharisees said, "What then? Are we blind, also?"

³ But Jesus told them, "If you were blind, you would be free of guilt. Yet because you claim to see, your guilt remains."

⁴ During these days, it is said that an old woman approached the group to hear him more fully, but she was pushed aside by one who was there to spy upon him. This one sought to block her from hearing his words, placing himself before her. ⁵ But Jesus told him, "It is not fitting

that a man should set aside his mother and take her place. Whoever respects not his mother, who is the most sacred being after his God, is unworthy to be called a son.

⁶ "Listen, therefore, to what I tell you: Respect woman, for she is the mother of the universe, and all the truth of divine creation lies within her. ⁷ She is the foundation of all that is good and beautiful, and she is the germ of life and death. On her depends man's entire existence, for she supports him both by her nature and her honor.

⁸ "Woman gives birth to a man in the midst of suffering and rears him by the sweat of her brow, enduring from him the greatest anxiety, even to her death. ⁹ Therefore do bless and exalt her, for she is your friend and supporter in this life. Respect her and honor her; in so acting, you will win her love and her heart. And you will find favor in the sight of God, with much forgiveness.

¹⁰ "In this way also, love and respect your own wives, for they will be mothers tomorrow. Offer them your forgiveness, for their love ennobles a man and softens his hardened heart, taming the brute in him so he becomes like a lamb. ¹¹ Your wife and your mother are priceless treasures bestowed by God. They are the fairest things in all existence, and of them shall be born the inhabitants of this world."

¹² They marveled at these words, for it seemed that he was exalting woman to make her the equal of man. ¹³ To this some men objected. Was it not Lilith who defied God and parted from Adam? And was it not Eve who tempted Adam in the garden? ¹⁴ Yet they forgot that it was Adam

who sought lordship over Lilith, who had been created as his equal, and it was Adam who sought to blame Eve for his own transgression.

[15] And they chafed at how he had rebuked them, seeking therefore a way to entrap him using guile.

Cast the First Stone

[16] One day, they brought him a woman who had been caught in lying with a man who was not her husband. They made her stand before the group that had gathered to hear Jesus, and they said, "Rabbi, this woman was found in the act of adultery. The law of Moses commands us to stone such a woman. What then do you say?"

[17] Jesus did not answer them directly, but instead bent down and began to write on the ground with his finger. (Now when a wise man seeks to invoke God's power or protection, he will draw a circle on the earth, as the righteous Honi had done when he brought rain to end a

great drought that was upon the land.)

[18] The men who were seeking to trap Jesus, however, continued to question him, so that he stood up and challenged them: "If any of you is without sin, let him be the first to cast a stone at her!" And he returned to writing on the ground.

[19] At this, those who had heard him began to depart that place one at a time, the older ones first, until only Jesus was left with her. [20] He therefore stood up again and asked her, "Woman, where are they? Has no one condemned you."

[21] "No one, sir," she said.

[22] "Then neither do I condemn you. Go your way and turn from your transgressions."

[23] Now a rumor arose that Jesus had stayed behind with her in arrogance, thinking he had not sinned. Yet he, too, refused to condemn the woman. This rumor was spread by his enemies in order to mock him and by his own followers who sought to exalt him, but Jesus himself remained silent and took no part in it.

Sons of Abraham

[24] Having failed in their purpose, his enemies sought to entrap him once again. And they came to him demanding to know on whose authority he was teaching.

[25] But he responded by asking them, "Was John's baptism from heaven or from men?"

[26] They therefore took counsel among themselves, but

they could not agree upon an answer. ²⁷ "If we say it was from heaven, he will ask us why we did not believe his words. But if we say it came from men, the people will stone us because they all thought John was a prophet." So they finally told him, "We do not know."

²⁸ Jesus therefore said to them, "Then neither will I tell you by what authority I am doing these things!"

²⁹ And he told them: "If you understood my teaching, you would know the truth, and the truth would set you free."

³⁰ "We are the sons of Abraham," they said. "We have never been slaves to anyone. How then can you say we will be set free?" ³¹ (In saying this, they betrayed their ignorance of the scripture, wherein the sons of Abraham enslaved to both the Egyptians and the Babylonians.)

³² Jesus replied: "I know you are sons of Abraham, yet you are ready to kill me because you have no place for my words. ³³ If you were Abraham's children, you would do the works of Abraham. As it is, you are determined to kill me for telling you the truth I heard from God. Abraham did no such thing."

³⁴ Being offended, his enemies grew angry with him and began to accuse him: "Are we not right in saying that you are a Samaritan and possessed by demons?" For they knew he had been doing wonders, healing those who were afflicted and curing those who were said to be possessed by demons. ³⁵ So they said to him, "You cast out demons by Beelzebul, who is the prince of demons!"

³⁶ Jesus therefore said to them, "A kingdom divided

against itself will be ruined, and a house divided is sure to fall. If Satan is divided against himself, how can his kingdom prevail? [37] If, therefore, I drive out demons by Beelzebul, by whom do your followers drive them out? But if I drive out demons by the finger of God, then the realm of God has come to you!"

[38] His adversaries failed to understand that all power comes from God, and that it falls upon the sons of men to use it wisely.

The Riddle of the Coin

[39] And they became all the more eager to entrap him, for his words were drawing even greater crowds to hear him. [40] So they came to him with false praise and said to him, "Teacher, we know that your teachings are correct, and that you show no partiality but teach the way of God in truth. Tell us, therefore, is it right for us to pay taxes to Caesar or not?"

[41] They asked him this knowing that many of his followers sought to make him a king (though he did not seek this for himself) so they might be free of Roman taxes. [42] If, therefore, he were to say "It is right," these men would declare him false and leave him. [43] If, to the contrary,

he were to say, "It is not right," his inquisitors would have grounds to arrest him for treason against the emperor.

⁴⁴ Jesus, however, knew their intentions.

⁴⁵ He therefore asked them, "Show me a denarius. Whose image does it bear?"

⁴⁶ And they produced the coin for his inspection. "The image of Caesar," they replied.

⁴⁷ So he said to them, "Then render to Caesar what is Caesar's and to God what belongs to God."

⁴⁸ They were astonished at his words, knowing that the coin indeed bore the image of Caesar but that all things belonged to God. And being unable to entrap him, they fell silent and went their way.

⁴⁹ Such men were those who accused him of fellowship with harlots and sinners, saying he had therefore become unclean. ⁵⁰ "John's disciples come fasting and praying," they said to him, "as do also the disciples of the Pharisees, yet yours come eating and drinking."

Parable of the Wineskins

⁵¹ But he answered them plainly, saying, "Would you compel the guests of the bridegroom to fast while he is among them? Yet the time will come when the bridegroom shall be removed from their presence, and in those days will they fast.

⁵² "No one tears a patch from a new garment and sews it onto an old one! If he does, the new garment will be ruined, and the patch he has taken from it will not match

the old. ⁵³ In the same way, no one pours new wine into old wineskins. If he does, the new wine will pour forth from the skins, and they also will be ruined. ⁵⁴ No, new wine must be poured into new wineskins. And no one who has partaken of the old wine wants the new, for he says, 'The old is better.' "

⁵⁵ This he said to them because he knew their hearts, that the teachers of the law would consult the scriptures and counsel men, saying "do this" or "do that" because it was written in the law and the prophets. ⁵⁶ They were like physicians who always prescribed the same treatment, neglecting to examine a single one who came to them infirm.

⁵⁷ They were drunk on old wine that had become like vinegar, while the new wine of each man's spirit was poured out as a sacrifice before them. ⁵⁸ And many toiled in vain seeking after a righteousness that was but falsehood, because the skins these so-called teachers had provided were poorly suited to their contents.

⁵⁹ "To what shall I compare this generation?" he said to them. "They are like children who sit in the marketplaces and call out to others: 'We played a flute for you, and you did not dance. We sang a dirge for you, yet you did not mourn.'

⁶⁰ "For John came neither eating nor drinking, and they say, 'He has a demon.' This son of man comes eating and drinking, and they say, 'He is a glutton and a drunkard, a friend of tax gatherers and sinners!' ⁶¹ Yet wisdom is vindicated by her actions."

[62] These men had no wisdom. They scorned her presence, resisted her entreaties, turned their back when she cried out to them, shunned the tears she cried for them.

[63] Therefore did Jesus condemn them.

Woes Against the Pharisees

[64] "You Pharisees clean the outside of a dish, but inside you are full of greed and strife. Fools! Did not the same one who made the outside of the dish make the inside also? But give what is inside the dish to the poor, and everything will be clean for you!

[65] "Woe to you scribes and Pharisees, hypocrites! You give God a tenth of your mint, rue and other garden herbs, yet neglect justice and the love of God! You blind guides! You strain out a gnat and swallow a camel!

⁶⁶ "Woe to you Pharisees, for you love the seats of honor in the synagogues and cherish the greetings you receive in the marketplace. Woe to you! You are like unmarked graves, which men tread upon unaware.

⁶⁷ "Woe to you scribes and Pharisees, hypocrites! You cross land and sea to make a single convert, and when this is accomplished, you make him twice as much of a son of hell as you are!"

⁶⁸ "Woe to you scribes and Pharisees, hypocrites! You are like whitewashed tombs that look beautiful on the outside but on the inside are filled with dead men's bones and all things unclean. You appear on the outside as blameless and good, but inside you are full of hypocrisy and bitterness.

⁶⁹ "And you experts in the law, woe to you! You load people down with burdens they can hardly bear, while you lift not one finger to aid them!

⁷⁰ "Woe to you who have no hope, who rely on things that will never come to pass!

⁷¹ "Woe to you caught in the fire that burns you, for it cannot be quenched. The wheel turns within your minds, yet you are hostage to the burning that is in you, which will devour your bodies openly and secretly consume your souls!"

⁷² "Woe to you who build tombs for the prophets, when it was your forefathers who killed them! You testify that you approve of what your forefathers did, yet they killed the prophets and you build their tombs! ⁷³ For this reason the wise God has said, 'I will send them prophets

and messengers, whom they will kill and persecute.'
⁷⁴ Therefore this generation will be responsible for the
blood of every prophet shed since the beginning of this
age!

⁷⁵ "Woe to you experts in the law, for you have hidden
the key to knowledge. You yourselves have not entered,
and you have hindered those who sought to enter!"

⁷⁶ And when he had spoken thus, he left that place and
returned again to Bethany.

17

¹ When the time came to reveal what was to come, Jesus took his disciples aside and told them plainly that he would be handed over to the authorities in Jerusalem and be killed, and that in three days he would rise again after the manner of his father, Osiris.

² His disciples were therefore grieved, wondering at what lay ahead once he had left them.

³ But he comforted them, saying, "Where two or more of you have gathered together, I am there in the midst of you. Behold, I am in all. Cleave the wood, and I am there. Lift a stone, and there you will find me."

⁴ And he told them this parable of a king and his servants, that the king would say to those who had been faithful: "Come you who are blessed of the father, inherit the kingdom that was prepared for you from the foundation of the world. For I hungered and you nourished me, I thirsted and you gave me drink, I was a stranger and you invited me in, I was naked and you clothed me, I was sick and you cared for me, I was imprisoned and you came to visit me."

⁵ For, he said, "whenever you do these things to the least of my brothers, you do them also for me. And whatever you do not do for the least of these, you likewise withhold from me."

⁶ "Be not troubled. Trust in God and also in me. In my father's house are many chambers. If it were not so, I would not have told you. ⁷ I go to prepare a place for you, and I will return to take you with me that you may join me there. You know the way to this place I speak of.

⁸ "If you love me, you will be glad that I go to the father, for the father is greater than I. ⁹ Believe me when I tell you that I am in the father and the father is in me. Truly I say to you that anyone who has faith will do what I have done and even greater things! ¹⁰ If you have faith as small as a mustard seed, you can say to a mulberry tree or even a mountain, 'Be uprooted and planted in the sea!' and it will obey you.

¹¹ These things he said to encourage them, but upon hearing them, Simon Peter took him aside to admonish him.

¹²Jesus therefore rebuked him, saying, "Are you my adversary? Get behind me! You do not consider the things of God, but only the concerns of men."

¹³He said these things because they knew not his intentions, which had been spoken of by the priesthood of the phoenix in Heliopolis. For he sought to present an example to them, that they should yield up everything and become servants of all.

¹⁴Therefore, he admonished them to humble themselves, saying, "The greatest among you will be your servant, for whosoever exalts himself will be humbled, but the one who acts in humility will be raised up."

Sacrifice You Did Not Desire

¹⁵Behold, he told them, "It is more blessed to give than to receive."

¹⁶Yet still they did not comprehend his words. And there arose a pernicious teaching that he meant to offer himself up as a sacrifice, and that this sacrifice would annul the sin of Adam. ¹⁷These men spread this teaching to many ears, not remembering the words of David: "Sacrifice and offering you did not desire. Neither did you desire burnt offerings or offerings for sin." ¹⁸Yet these false messengers, regarding themselves as wise teachers, polluted the message of Jesus by saying that he came to be a sin offering – a thing which God did not desire!

¹⁹For it is not through burnt offerings and sacrifices that sins are atoned for, but this comes alone through love

and faithfulness. As it is written:

> ²⁰ To what purpose do you offer me these multitudes of
>   sacrifice?
> ²¹ I have had enough of your burnt offerings of rams
>   And the bloated fat of your cattle
> ²² I delight not in the blood of bulls or lambs or goats
> ²³ He who kills a bull is as if he slays a man
>   And he who sacrifices a lamb
>   as if he breaks the neck of a dog

²⁴ Let the reader therefore heed the words of the
prophet who said, "I desire mercy, not a sacrifice," and
listen not to these men who flout the scripture. ²⁵ For
mercy is not paid for with a sacrifice, but rather is freely
given. ²⁶ Does a judge show mercy if he is paid to render a

verdict? Or is such a one corrupt and without justice? [27] Does a ruler show mercy if he is bribed to provide favors? Or is such a one far from the light? [28] As it is written: "The wicked man accepts a bribe in secret and so perverts the course of justice" And again: "Woe to those who acquit the guilty for a bribe, yet deny justice to the innocent."

[29] Yet Jesus said, "Blessed are the merciful, for these shall be shown mercy."

[30] He therefore told this parable: "A man was traveling from Jerusalem to Jericho, when he fell into the hands of robbers. These men stripped him of his clothes, beat him and went on their way, leaving him half-dead. [31] A priest who was traveling this same road saw the man, but passed by on the far side. In the same way, a Levite came upon the man but also passed by on the far side.

[32] "Yet a Samaritan, when he came to where the man lay, took pity on him. He went to him and bandaged his wounds, pouring oil and wine on them. He put the man on his own donkey, took him to the inn and cared for him. [33] The following day, he gave two silver coins to the innkeeper, saying, "Look after him, and when I return, I will pay you for any extra expenses you may have."

[34] And Jesus asked an expert in the law which of the three men showed the victim mercy.

[35] And the man answered and said to him, "The one who showed him mercy."

[36] Jesus therefore told him, "Go therefore and do likewise."

18

¹ Now Jesus knew that the Sanhedrin was seeking to arrest him and had been prevented from doing so only by the crowds. So he spoke to some of his followers inside the city, who sought out a place where he might partake of the Passover meal in peace. ² When this was concluded, he knew, he would no longer be able to forestall what lay before him. ³ He therefore called his brother Judas and instructed him to prepare for his arrest, discussing these things with him in secret, knowing that others would seek to prevent it.

⁴ He told his disciples, "When you enter the city, a man

bearing a jar of water will come to meet you. Follow this one and enter that house which he enters. ⁵ Say to the owner of the house, 'The rabbi asks: Where is the guest room, that I may eat the Passover with my disciples?' ⁶ He will show you to a large upper room, which is furnished. Prepare yourselves there."

⁷ They found everything as he had arranged it.

⁸ When the meal was served, he rose from the table and removed his outer clothing, wrapping his waist in a towel and pouring some water into a basin. He then began to wash his disciples' feet, using the towel to dry them.

⁹ But his brother Simon protested, saying, "Surely you will not wash my feet!"

¹⁰ Jesus answered and said to him, "You know not what I am doing, but you will come to understand. Unless I wash you, you will have no part of me."

¹¹ Simon then adjured him to wash his entire body.

¹² But Jesus said, "The one who has bathed need only wash his feet; then shall his entire body be clean. ¹³ Now that I have washed your feet, you also should wash one another's. I have set this as an example for you, and you will be blessed if you follow it."

¹⁴ Then he took bread and broke it, saying, "Behold, my body shall be broken for you. Whenever you break bread, remember me." ¹⁵ And he took the cup and blessed it, saying, "Behold, this cup shall be as a covenant of my blood, which I will pour out for you. I tell you truly, I will not again drink of the fruit of the vine until I drink it anew with you in the kingdom of my father."

¹⁶ Then James said to him that he would therefore not break bread again until Jesus should complete that which must be done.

¹⁷ And Jesus said, "Even now the hand of he who will betray me is at the table. This son of man shall go as has been decreed, but woe to the one who shall betray him."

¹⁸ And they all began to murmur among themselves, questioning who among them he might mean.

¹⁹ Simon spoke up, saying, "I am willing to endure prison or even die for you!"

²⁰ But Jesus said, "Truly I tell you, before the rooster crows this day you will deny me three times over!"

²¹ Then, when the meal was nearly finished, Jesus handed Judas a piece of bread, which was a signal, saying, "What you must do, do quickly."

²² Judas departed.

²³ And the story arose among them that it was Judas who would betray him, though Judas acted according to Jesus' own instruction.

²⁴ It was to Simon, however, that he spoke this warning: "Simon, our adversary has asked to sift you like wheat. I pray for you, my brother, that your faith does not fail you and, when you have returned to your senses, that you strengthen your brothers." ²⁵ For Simon was a Zealot whose wish was to conquer by the sword, having not understood when Jesus admonished him to turn the other cheek. ²⁶ And it was Simon, not Judas, who would deny him.

Gethsemane

²⁷ So it was that they left that place and went forth to the Mount of Olives. But Judas went to the chief priests and officers of the temple guard and, drawing them aside, proposed to deliver Jesus into their hands. ²⁸ This assistance they accepted gladly, having sought a way for some time to arrest Jesus in solitude, away from the multitudes who followed him. ²⁹ Jesus, though, knew well their intentions, though they knew not that he had commissioned Judas to speak with them.

³⁰ For Judas alone among his brothers had understood

when he said, "Resist not your enemy." [31] Simon had proclaimed him messiah, the savior sent to deliver Israel from the bonds of the Roman occupation. He and many others had sought to crown him king of an earthly realm.

[32] Yet time and again he had refused them, and now he would refuse them yet again. [33] These were a hard-hearted people, but perhaps they might learn through the power of example. For he told them, "Greater love has no man than this, that he should lay his life down for his friends."

[34] Some therefore thought he meant to die, yet he sought only the death of desire that begins in meekness and blossoms into servanthood. For service is the fruit of humility, and such is the way of the Therapeutae.

[35] Jesus knew the authorities were determined to arrest him, and he lacked any means to prevent it. [36] He would therefore yield himself up of his own accord, so that all things might be fulfilled and that he might be delivered. As it is written: "He crowns me with deliverance."

[37] And again: "Pride walks boldly to its own destruction, and a spirit of arrogance leads to a fall. Far better it is to be oppressed and be humble in spirit than to share the plunder with men of conceit."

[38] And as he himself had taught them, "Whoever exalts himself will be humbled, but the one who humbles himself is raised up."

[39] For he knew this must be fulfilled: that he be raised up on the cross of the phoenix and be reborn, just as the great father Osiris was reborn from days of old. [40] Now, as he had raised Simon the Pharisee as Osiris from the tomb

in Bethany, so he too would be raised from the tomb to a new life. [41] There were men on the council, he knew, who could assist him in this purpose: one Joseph, a wealthy man from Arimathea who counted himself among Jesus' disciples; and a friend named Nicodemus.

[42] It was Nicodemus whom he had counseled that truly, "no man can behold the realm of God unless he is born anew."

[43] "How can a man be born when he is old?" Nicodemus had objected. "Surely he cannot enter a second time into his mother's womb!"

[44] But Jesus had said, "Behold, I tell you truly that no one can enter the realm of God unless he is born of water and the spirit. Flesh gives birth to flesh, but the spirit gives birth to spirit. [45] You should not marvel that I say, 'You must be born anew.' For the wind blows wherever it pleases. You hear the sound, but you cannot say whence it comes or where it flies. So it is with everyone born of the spirit."

[46] He had spoken of his mother, the spirit of wisdom. And Nicodemus had understood. Jesus therefore told him, "Just as Moses lifted up the serpent in the desert, so must this son of man be lifted up."

[47] For it is written that serpents came against the children of Israel in the desert, and Moses fashioned an image of bronze after their likeness and raised it up upon his staff. [48] And it is said that whoseover had been bitten by one of the serpents could look upon the image Moses created and live.

⁴⁹ The serpent was an image of wisdom, and like the phoenix was a sign of the second birth, for it shed it skin to appear renewed.

⁵⁰ Now Jesus would likewise be renewed, setting an example for all who were to follow: "If anyone wishes to come after me, he must deny himself and take up his cross. For whoever wants to save his life will lose it, but whoever loses his life because of me and my words shall find it. ⁵¹ Indeed, what does it profit a man if he gains the whole world yet forfeits his soul? What can a man give in exchange for his soul? ⁵² If any man be ashamed of me and my words, this son of man will likewise be ashamed of him before the father."

⁵³ These words he spoke also to foretell the fate of Simon Peter, whose bold declarations of faithfulness would soon give way to shame.

Jesus Arrested

⁵⁴ Now, however, did Peter and the others go out with him to the Mount of Olives on the eastern side of the city, and to the garden that was called Gethsemane at the base of it. ⁵⁵ Here, he knew, Judas would find him and bring his enemies to arrest him if all went according to plan. So he took Simon Peter and two others with him to stand watch as he made ready to pray, telling them, "My soul is grieved to the point of death. Remain here and keep watch with me."

⁵⁶ He went on farther and prayed, but returning, found them asleep.

⁵⁷ "Can you not even keep watch with me one hour?" he asked them. "The spirit is willing, but how the flesh is weak!"

⁵⁸ And shortly afterward there was a commotion, and a large crowd of men armed with swords and clubs appeared, led by the men on the council and Judas alongside them.

⁵⁹ Jesus therefore greeted him, saying, "My friend, do what you have come for."

⁶⁰ Judas stepped forward and kissed him in greeting, whereupon the others laid hands upon him to arrest him.

⁶¹ But Simon Peter, drawing a sword, lashed out in force at the high priest's servant so that his ear was cut off. Even now he failed to comprehend, seeking to establish a kingdom by force of arms. ⁶² Yet Jesus rebuked him. "Lay down your sword!" he said. "For all who draw the sword will likewise perish by the sword."

⁶³ Then he turned to the mass of people assembled there and said to them, "Am I leading a rebellion, that you come forth with swords and clubs to capture me? Each day I sat in the temple courts teaching, yet still you did not arrest me."

⁶⁴ But they held him fast.

⁶⁵ Now a young man wearing nothing but a linen garment had been following Jesus. ⁶⁶ Catching sight of him, some in the crowd sought now to seize him, yet he escaped them and fled, leaving the garment behind in his haste. And so did the rest of his disciples do likewise, though Simon Peter followed at a distance behind him.

19

¹ They brought Jesus to the house of the high priest, though it was late in the evening and the council met formally only in daylight. ² Still, they were determined to question him and find evidence against him that was worthy of death. So they assembled in that place, all the chief priests and elders and members of the council with them, along with the high priest, whose name was Caiaphas. ³ These brought any number of witnesses to speak against him, but they could come to no decision, for their statements did not agree.

^{4} At last two men came forward and said, "We heard this man say he was able to destroy the temple of God and rebuild it again in three days."

^{5} The high priest demanded that Jesus answer the charge, but he remained silent.

^{6} Now while these things were happening, a crowd of people had gathered outside, and when some among them lit a fire in the courtyard, Simon Peter came to sit amongst them. ^{7} But a servant girl caught sight of him and began to look closely at him. Then she said, "This man was with them."

^{8} Yet he denied it, saying, "Woman, I know him not."

^{9} Shortly afterward, another among their number spied him and accused him: "You are one of them."

^{10} But he denied it again, saying, "Man, I am not!" And he moved away from them to stand in the entryway.

^{11} An hour had passed when yet another spoke up and said, "Certainly this man here was with him, for he is a Galilean."

^{12} Simon therefore began to curse and denied it: "Man, I know not what you are about!" ^{13} But at that moment, a cock crowed, and Jesus turned to look at Simon where he stood watching in the doorway so that he remembered the words spoken to him only hours before: "Before the rooster crows this day, you will deny me three times."

^{14} And Peter moved away, going from that place.

^{15} Yet inside ,they persisted in their questioning, asking Jesus directly: "Are you the messiah, son of the blessed one?"

¹⁶ But he told them only, "Those are your words."

¹⁷ Yet they deemed the testimony sufficient to condemn him, and they ordered him bound and taken to Pontius Pilate, the Roman prefect in Jerusalem, that he might pass judgment.

Before Pilate

¹⁸ Now Pilate was known among the people for his cruelty and inflexible disposition. Not long before, he had earned the enmity of the people by bringing images of Caesar into the holy city, where it is unlawful to set up any graven image. ¹⁹ He set them up in the city under cover of darkness, so as not to inflame the people, yet when they saw them, there arose a clamor and the men of that city came before Pilate to petition for their removal.

²⁰ But Pilate, not wishing to grant their request for fear of offending Caesar, instructed his soldiers to surround them and call death down upon them should they resist him. ²¹ Yet instead, they bared their necks to him and cast themselves upon the earth, saying they would willingly suffer death rather than see the laws of their fathers so transgressed. ²² And Pilate, being vexed, removed the images from their presence and returned them to Caesarea, whence they had come.

²³ No sooner had this crisis passed than another arose to take its place. For Pilate, seeking to build an aqueduct to bring water into Jerusalem, made use of money from the temple fund to do so. ²⁴ The people therefore, being

offended, gathered together in a crowd and began to hurl abuses at him for this act, insisting that he should set aside his program.

²⁵ But he, growing weary with them, set among the crowd his own men armed with daggers beneath their vestments. And at a signal, they withdrew their weapons and set themselves against the crowd in vengeance, sparing neither the unarmed nor the innocent.

²⁶ A great number of men were slain that day, and the rest were put to rout, in which manner Pilate brought an end to their sedition.

²⁷ Pilate's disposition in these matters bode auspiciously for Jesus' accusers that he might act in the same manner now against their prisoner.

²⁸ Bringing him therefore before the prefect, Jesus' enemies told Pilate, "This man subverts our nation by opposing Caesar's taxes and claiming to be the messiah, a king. He was born of fornication and deceives the people by means of sorcery. Were he not a criminal, we would not have brought him here to you."

²⁹ "Take him, then, and judge him by your own laws," Pilate told them, but they objected, saying "It is not permitted for us to put a man to death."

³⁰ So Pilate withdrew to the palace and summoned Jesus to him, asking, "Are you the king of the Jews?"

³¹ Jesus said: "Is that your idea, or did others say this of me?"

³² "Am I a Jew?" Pilate scoffed. "It is your own countrymen who have delivered you up to me. Tell me,

therefore, what it is that you have done."

³³ But Jesus said, "My kingdom is not of this world. Were it so, those who follow me would have fought to prevent my arrest. Yet my kingdom is from another place. I was born and came into this world to testify of truth, for which reason everyone on the side of truth marks my words.

³⁴ "What is truth?" Pilate asked him.

³⁵ And he went back out to the people and told them, "I find no grounds to charge this man." ³⁶ But they persisted, saying, "This man stirs up people all across Judea with his teaching. He came out of Galilee and now has come down here!"

Jesus Acquitted

[37] Now upon hearing that Jesus was from Galilee, Pilate sought to be rid of the matter by transferring it to Antipas, the tetrarch of that region and who had come to Jerusalem for the Passover.

[38] Antipas for his part was greatly pleased at the sight of Jesus, for he had wanted to speak with him for some time and hoped to see him perform a great wonder. He asked him many things, but Jesus remained silent and answered not, so his soldiers, mocking, dressed him in a grand robe and sent him back to Pilate.

[39] The prefect therefore summoned the members of the council before him and told them, "You brought me this man accused of fomenting a rebellion, yet I have examined him before you and found no basis for your charges against him. Likewise has Antipas sent him back here, finding also that he has done nothing deserving death. I will therefore scourge him and release him."

[40] But a crowd had gathered, and there arose a great commotion. Some among them cried, "Away with him!" Yet others said, "Release to us Barabbas!" (which means "son of the father," a name Jesus had used for himself – for many among them were pleading that he might be released).

[41] And other voices still arose, shouting, "Crucify him!" [42] And the rabble would not be stilled, even though Pilate urged them to silence. [43] But while Pilate was seated there, a courier arrived with a message from his wife, saying,

"Have nothing to do with this innocent man, for in a dream today I was sorely afflicted because of him."

[44] So Pilate stood and took a basin of water, dipped his hands in and washed them in front of the entire crowd. "I am innocent of this man's blood!" he declared. "Do with him what you will." [45] And he ordered him flogged, then surrendering him to their will.

20

¹ Joseph of Arimathea was a member of the council who esteemed the teachings of Jesus. ² He therefore went to Pilate and asked him to take custody of the Galilean. And he took him forth from that place as the crowd followed after. ³ Among these were some women who lamented him, and he said to them, "Daughters of Jerusalem, weep not for me, but for yourselves and for your children. Behold, the day is coming when it shall be said, 'Blessed are the wombs that never bore and the breasts that never nursed.' ⁴ Then shall the sons of men cry out to the mountains, saying, 'Fall on us!' and beseech the

hills, saying, 'Cover us!' For if they do these things when the tree is green, what more will they do when it has withered?"

⁵At length they came to a parcel of land belonging to Joseph called Golgotha, which means "place of the skull" and had, in days of old, been home to Aphrodite's temple. ⁶So it was that he returned now to the place of his mother in spirit, the great goddess known also as Isis, to take up the mantle of the phoenix, which is the cross.

⁷As it is written, "I am naught but dust and ashes." Yet it was from these ashes that the phoenix would arise anew.

⁸All this was to be done according to his own plan. As it was written by the prophet Job, whose life was taken from him but returned in greater measure:

⁹O, for the days of my prime
   When God was a friend who blessed my house
   When the Almighty was yet with me
   And my children did surround me
¹⁰When my path was bathed in cream
   And the rocks poured forth olive oil in streams
   When I went to gate of the city
   And took my seat in the public square
¹¹I rescued the poor who cried out helpless
   And the orphan with none to assist him
   The dying man blessed me
   And the widow's heart sang
¹²I clothed myself in virtue
   With justice my robe and headpiece

I was eyes to the blind and feet to the lame
A father to the needy and an advocate for the
stranger
[13] I broke the fangs of the wicked
Snatching victims from their teeth
I said to myself, "I will die in my own nest
And my days shall be as the days of the phoenix"

[14] Now some men say that the Romans crucified Jesus, but they know not what they say. For Pilate, finding no guilt in him, released him. [15] And others began to murmur against the Jews, saying his blood was on their children. But these, too, are in error. For did not the leaders of the council say, "It is not lawful for us to put a man to death"? Nor would they have crucified a man, but would have stoned him, as commanded in the law.

[16] It was therefore his own followers who believed in him that took him forth to the place of death and renewal, where he would be raised up as the phoenix, a symbol of life eternal.

The Phoenix Raised Up

[17] So they put him on a cross and raised it up there. It was the third hour of the day.

[18] Some came to offer him wine mixed with myrrh, but he refused it. And there stood at the foot of the cross Mary Magdalene, with his mother and his mother's sister, the wife of Clopas, and also Salome.

¹⁹ And it came to pass that, at the sixth hour, the sky was darkened and the sun removed from their sight until the ninth hour, just as the skies are darkened in the depths of winter, when the sun descends to its nether point on the horizon and dwells there three days before ascending.

²⁰ Jesus therefore cried out, "Eloi! Eloi! Lama sabachthani!" which translated means, "My god! My god! Why have you forsaken me?"

²¹ Someone ran to get him drink and offered it to him at the end of a hyssop branch. Now some say it this was wine vinegar, yet surely it was not, for he had pledged to his disciples, "I will not drink again from the fruit of the vine again until the day I drink it anew with you in the realm of my father." ²² Yet when he drank it, he declared, "It is finished!"

²³ And they pierced him with a spear, as it is written in the Book of Going Forth By Day. For the gatekeeper of the fifth portal in death is "the one who spears the disaffected." ²⁴ When they did this, blood and water poured forth from his wound, for he yet lived, even as he journeyed through the gates of the underworld. This was a marvel of marvels.

²⁵ So they took him down from there and salved his wounds with spices, and they wrapped him in linen cloths. ²⁶ And Joseph took him to the tomb hewn from out of rock which was to be his own, and laid him there in a garden, at the place he had been crucified.

²⁷ And Mary Magdalene was there in that place also, with Mary who was his mother. At length these two

departed to prepare spices and ointments, that they might minister to him.

The Empty Tomb

[28] And they rested on the Sabbath, but on the third day, before it was light, they returned to the place where he had been laid and found the tomb disturbed, and Jesus was no longer there. [29] At this they were vexed. But they spied a young man in white, sitting beside the tomb, one of his disciples who had been appointed to stand watch. [30]And he said to them, "Do not be dismayed. You seek Jesus, who was crucified. But he has arisen."

³¹ Mary Magdalene went forth from that place and found his brothers John and Simon Peter, declaring to them, "They have taken away my lord, and I know not where they have laid him." ³² She said this in a mystery, for she had known of his intentions. For just as Isis had searched for her slain consort Osiris in days of old, she now would take up the mantle of the goddess and search for her fallen husband who was taken from her.

³³ But the men were disbelieving, for Jesus had not told them of his plans lest they prevent him. Therefore did they make haste to Joseph's garden and, finding the tomb, found it all as she had said, with only the linen cloths left lying there. ³⁴ So they went away to their own homes, leaving Mary there alone beside the tomb, weeping, for she was afraid.

³⁵ And a voice from behind came to her, saying, "Woman, why do you weep?"

³⁶ She therefore turned to see Jesus, who appeared to her as the gardener, which is the title of Osiris. At first, she did not recognize him, but then he spoke her name to her.

"Mary."

³⁷ And at once she knew him and ran forth to hold him, crying, "My teacher!"

³⁸ Now Jesus went forth to James, who had sworn that he should not eat bread again until he should see Jesus risen from among those who sleep. ³⁹ So therefore Jesus came to him, saying, "Bring a table and some bread!" ⁴⁰ And he took the bread and broke it, and gave it to James, saying, "My brother, partake of your bread, for this son of

man has risen from among those who sleep!"

⁴¹ During this time, Mary also went her way, and she ran to tell his followers that Jesus was alive, but they did not believe her. (For they did not know that Joseph was a friend to Jesus, and they believed he had acted as a member of the council in taking him away, that he might be killed). ⁴² Now two other men also came to them, reporting that they, too, had seen him. ⁴³ Jesus had come also after them, and in that moment he arrived to stand among them. ⁴⁴ But the disciples were terrified, for they believed that they were seeing a ghost.

⁴⁵ He therefore said to them, "Why are you troubled? Why do doubts arise within your hearts? Look now upon my hands, and on my feet, and see that it is truly I. Touch me and see, for a ghost has neither flesh nor bone as I have."

⁴⁶ And he asked them, "Have you anything to eat?"

⁴⁷ They brought him a broiled fish and some honeycomb, whereupon he ate them in their presence.

⁴⁸ So it was for him as it had been for Osiris, who proclaimed:

I am yesterday, the dawn and tomorrow
    I oversee the rebirth of souls, of all nature
    And her mysteries
⁴⁹ I am the Creator of the gods
    Who nourish the hosts of heaven,
    They that inhabit the Western sky
⁵⁰ I am the master of the East, I have two faces

I arrange the rising of the sun,
Whose rays rise up into the sky
And which descends at dawn
To transform the dwellings of the dead
[51] Abundance is my name: I am generous,
Yet my true self is hidden
I am the ray of light which appears at your door
And goes where it will
[52] I supply every need of the blest,
Sending forth blessing in vessels beyond number
[53] I am in charge of this wealth,
Bestowed according to its time
On the day when we shall see
The companions of Orion,
Of whom there number twelve
[54] I came to Heliopolis
To tell the phoenix about what passes in heaven
[55] Let me rise up and see the light of the sun
Let me travel in peace
And walk upon the celestial waters
[56] Let me fly toward the splendor of the blest,
Toward Ra who gives life
Anew each day to everyone
[57] I am Osiris, whose name is owner
Of lands beyond measure
I embraced the sycamore and she did protect me
The doors of heaven opened for me
[58] I went to see Ra at his setting
I was one with the wind when he returned

My hands were purified in adoring him,
Yet I can do all that the living do
⁵⁹ I was resurrected,
I flew up to the sky and I rested on earth
My eyes saw what I wished to see
⁶⁰ I am the one who brought into the world
The One who knows the plan for life on earth
And in the kingdom of the dead

Doubting Thomas

⁶¹ Now Judas Thomas, who had delivered him at Gethsemane, was not there with them when he came to them, for he dared not risk coming close to him again for fear of the authorities. ⁶² When, therefore, the others told him that Jesus had returned, he would not credit them, for he had been filled with doubt that Jesus would succeed in his intentions. ⁶³ And he said to them, "Unless I see the scars upon his hands and touch his side where the spear did pierce him, I will not believe."

⁶⁴ So it was that eight days later, Jesus returned to meet with them again. ⁶² Now the doors had been locked, so only those with the proper key could enter. But Jesus, arriving in their midst, greeted them, saying, "Peace be upon you." ⁶⁵ And he said to Thomas, "Stretch forth your fingers and see my hands. Reach out your hand and touch my side. Now do you believe?"

⁶⁶ Judas, seeing that he was alive, cried out to heaven, "My lord and my God!"

[67] And Jesus said to him, "Because you have seen me, you have believed. Blessed are those who believe without seeing."

[68] So it was that Jesus fulfilled all things that are given a son of heaven to fulfill, and he did so in a mystery, a baptism and anointing. [69] The mystery was the mystery of birth and everlasting. The baptism was the wonder of new birth. The anointing was the work of Magdalene. [70] So also did he fulfill all things in a feast, which is the bridegroom's, and in a sacrifice, which is the death of self, and in the bridal chamber, which is the holy of holies.

[71] These things have been written that you may believe in the realm of God which is unseen. [72] It is not found in books or temples or laws laid down by men. For will God really make his dwelling on the earth, when even the highest heaven cannot contain him? Will he really dwell in a temple made by human hands, or in words on a printed page? [73] But the words of God are written on your hearts, for the realm of God resides within you and in every fiber of creation. [74] This realm is one, just as God is One. And just as Jesus became a child of heaven, so you may also be.

[75] Blessed is the one who adds to what has been written here with the fruit of his own life.

Selah.

Author's commentary

The preceding text contains various excerpts that are familiar from the Christian New Testament. But it also includes stories and quotes from a large number sources that were excluded from the canon and actively suppressed by what came to be the "official" church.

It isn't commonly known that a wealth of material about Jesus exists outside the four canonical gospels. Much of this has come to light in recent decades, including a treasure trove of Gnostic texts uncovered at Nag Hammadi in Egypt. The most well-known Gnostic gospel is a selection of 113 sayings attributed to Jesus known as the Gospel of Thomas. Sometimes referred to as the "fifth gospel," it contains little biographical information and has more in common with the Tao te Ching in terms of format than it does with, say, the Gospel of Mark. It's a collection of sayings, with only bare-bones context, where context exists at all. As such, it may be similar to the now-lost text scholars call "Q": a collection of sayings found in both

Matthew and Luke, but missing from Mark.

These three gospels together are called the Synoptics, from syn- (same) and -optic (sight). Mark was written first, with Matthew and Luke having used much of the material from the "Q" text in their own compositions. John, however, has little in common with the other three and was produced independently. Interestingly, however, some of the sayings found in the canonical texts are also found (and sometimes expanded upon) in Thomas. Here's one example:

- Luke: "The realm of God is not something that can be seen, nor will people say, 'It is here' or 'It is there,' for the realm of God is within you."

- Thomas: "If your leaders say to you, 'Behold, the kingdom is in the sky,' then the birds of the sky will precede you. If they say to you, 'It is in the sea,' then the fish will precede you. But rather, the kingdom is within you, and it is all around you."

Thomas includes the bit about the fish of the sea and the birds of the sky, driving home the point that the realm to which Jesus referred was not a physical kingdom, but rather one of the spirit.

Other texts, less well known than Thomas, also circulated among the Gnostics, were also widely distributed during the first three centuries of the common era before coming under increasing pressure from what came to be "mainstream" Christianity. It's important to remember, though, that there was really no such thing as "mainstream"

Christianity during the first three centuries. Instead, there were several competing traditions of Jesus' life and purpose, each of which produced its own literature.

The Gnostics were largely dualists who believed that the fleshly or physical realm was merely a cage created to imprison the pure spirit of the true god. Many Gnostics held that the physical world had been created by an inferior being known as the Demiurge. This inferior creator was viewed as an evil jailer who had constructed the corrupt physical universe to enslave the pure spirit that issued forth from the true (higher) creator.

Like other Christians, the Gnostics revered Jesus, but unlike them, they did not believe he had come "in the flesh," but rather in a non-corporeal body of pure spirit. As a result, many believed, he only appeared to have lived a normal human life and suffered on the cross. Because of this belief, they became known as Docetists, a term related to Greek words for phantom, apparition and illusion.

Some have argued that Paul, the author of several canonical epistles or letters, held some Gnostic views of his own, especially when it comes to his discussions of an apparent dichotomy between the sinful flesh and the righteous spirit. Others have seen signs of Gnostic influence in the Gospel of John.

In addition to the Gospel of Thomas, Gnostic writings included the Gospels of Philip and Mary (Magdalene), both of which have been used as source materials for this book. Other Gnostic texts dealing with the person of Jesus include the recently discovered Gospel of Judas, the

Dialogue of the Savior and the Apocryphon of James.

Groups beside the Gnostics flourished during the centuries following Jesus' time, whose members held beliefs that varied and weren't consistent with Pauline Christianity, which came to be the dominant form following the Council of Nicea in 325 CE. One of these groups was the Ebionites, literally "the Poor," who had a far more traditionally Jewish view of Jesus. They didn't believe that he was a divine son of their god, but rather that he was a human messiah, literally an "anointed one." Unlike Paul and his followers, they insisted that Jewish customs concerning such matters as diet and circumcision be followed. They believed that salvation came through good works, not faith or merely believing in Jesus' divinity (which they, in any case rejected). As a result, they came into conflict with Paul and his followers, a conflict that plays out in the canonical epistles and the Acts of the Apostles if one knows where to look.

Some argued for excluding the Epistle of James from the New Testament on the grounds that its author contradicted Paul's doctrine that divine acceptance was contingent upon faith alone, by grace. The author of James, however, challenged this view directly: "Someone will say, 'You have faith; I have works.' Therefore show me your faith without works, and I will show you my faith by my works." The unnamed "someone" could well have been Paul. The Epistle of James is, in fact, attributed to Jesus' brother by that name (Hebrew: Jacob). James is depicted in Acts as the first leader of the movement following Jesus' death; he is also acknowledged as such by Paul, albeit grudgingly, in the Epistle to the Galatians.

Jewish-Christian literature that seems to have been circulating in the first few centuries included a Gospel of the Ebionites, a Gospel of the Nazarenes, and a Gospel of the Hebrews. All exist only in fragmentary sayings preserved by opponents who may have had a hand in seeing them destroyed. Material from the Gospel of the Hebrews is quoted in this work and identifies James as the first person to see Jesus after the crucifixion.

Other material on James is included in the so-called Recognitions of Clement, a text that appears to be an Ebionite answer to the Acts of the Apostles, composed at a somewhat later date. James is also mentioned by the Roman Jewish historian Josephus.

The belief that Christianity sprang fully formed, in its current state, from the life and teachings of Jesus, simply cannot be sustained. Because so many people view the New Testament as a unified work, rather than a collection of writings, there's a tendency for it all to bleed together. Teachings of Paul, for example, are often attributed to Jesus, even though there's no evidence that Jesus had anything to say about many of the subjects Paul mentions. Such distinctions, however, are too often lost on those who view the Bible as "infallible." After all, it's a waste of time to look for contradictions or inconsistencies if you believe, from the outset, that they aren't an option.

The fact is, however, that several different proposed canons were floating around before the one we have today became the standard. The Muratorian Canon, for example, accepted the Revelation of Peter, which was ultimately excluded. The Syrian church, meanwhile, omitted the short epistle attributed to Jude, the second and third epistles of John, the Revelation of John and the second epistle of Peter.

Another list, contained on a document called the Codex Sinaiticus, contained the Epistle of Barnabas and the Shepherd of Hermas. Other works frequently read in early churches, with clerical approval, included the Didache (also known as the Teaching of the Twelve Apostles) and the First Epistle of Clement.

Some versions of the Latin Vulgate canon include the Epistle to the Laodiceans, a text attributed to (but not written by) Paul. Indeed, most modern scholars agree that Paul himself only wrote seven of the thirteen canonical texts attributed to him. The Epistle to the Hebrews, once considered Pauline, is no longer regarded as such even within the church, and its authorship is unknown.

Gnostic teachers, meanwhile, had their own collections.

Things were not nearly as simple as they might seem to the modern eye, which is accustomed to a stable canon and a fairly uniform doctrine.

By contrast, there were many Jesus movements in the first few centuries of the common era, and none claimed supremacy until the Emperor Constantine threw his weight behind what now is recognized as "orthodoxy." In other words, there were no heretics in the early years, merely competing visions. One group considered Mary the

"Mother of God," while another denied this view. One group acknowledged the trinity, while another, the Arians, stood firmly behind the idea of a single, indivisible deity. To them, the idea of a trinity was nothing less than a return to polytheism, something they could not accept. The monophysites believed that Jesus had a single "nature," but the fourth ecumenical council at Chalcedon declared in 451 CE that he had two: divine and human.

Just as many different ideas emerged in the years following Jesus' death, many ideas undoubtedly influenced his philosophy. Galilee, where Jesus was born, was called Galilee of the Gentiles for a reason: Not only wasn't it exclusively Jewish, it was extremely cosmopolitan. Its capital city, Sepphoris, was barely a couple of miles from Nazareth, the city referred to in the canon as Jesus' hometown.

As the regional capital, Sepphoris stood at an important crossroads between an east-west highway from the Mediterranean coast to the Sea of Galilee and a north-south route that came up from Jerusalem. Not only did it have a synagogue, but also a (pagan) Roman theater. A villa unearthed by archaeologists shows a mosaic devoted to the Roman god of the vine, Dionysus and containing images of other pagan figures: Pan and Hercules. Jesus would have doubtless been exposed to these gods and many others during trips to the city.

Jesus' time spent in Egypt is touched on briefly in the canon and discussed at greater length below, as well as in my book The Phoenix Principle. It is hard to imagine him and his parents not being exposed to the Egyptian mysteries, especially those of Isis, whose cult was among the most widespread around the Mediterranean in Jesus' time. Many of her attributes were later transferred to Jesus' own mother as she gained prominence in the centuries to come. (In fact, the images of Madonna and child that became ubiquitous in Christian traditions are clearly modeled after images of Isis and the infant Horus suckling at her breast, which may have been nearly as ubiquitous themselves in Jesus' day.)

The similarities between Jesus' life and the Egyptian myths of Horus, Isis and the "heavenly father" Osiris are remarkable, and some of them are laid out in this work. To what extent did Jesus consciously model his life after these myths, and to what extent did later writers use them as a means of constructing their own myths about him? The precise answer to this is impossible to know. There are those who believe the entire story of Jesus is a myth itself, and that no one by that name even existed. At the other end of the spectrum are those who believe that Jesus did everything contained in the canon, and that those texts constitute an unassailably accurate account of a historical individual's life.

The truth probably lies somewhere in between. It's extremely unusual for people set in historical contexts to be invented out of whole cloth and presented as real people … especially when their lives contain so much specific and vivid detail. Narratives tend to be of two sorts. Some concern gods, whose activities take place largely in the heavenly realms (with occasional visits to earth on the side). The Greek gods live on Olympus and, while they meddle in human affairs, there's a certain ethereal and timeless quality to their narratives. The second type of story concerns aggrandized human figures. These are real people whose stories are embellished, because of their high status or heroic reputations. While they have their roots in history, their followers describe them in godlike or mythic terms. Apollonius of Tyana, a wonder worker who was a near-contemporary of Jesus, is one example. The deified Roman emperors are another. Jesus, I would argue, also falls into this category.

I specifically chose to exclude accounts of Jesus' purported miraculous exploits from The Gospel of the Phoenix, because I think they're likely to be the same sort of embellishments. The exceptions are acts of healing, which could be attributed to his expertise in as a physician in the tradition of the Therapeutae. This isn't too farfetched. At one point, in the Gospel of Luke, Jesus predicts that his opponents will quote a specific proverb to him: "Physician, heal yourself." This seems to have indicated that they viewed him in precisely this light. Nature miracles such as walking on water, calming the seas and so forth aren't mentioned here, simply because they seem unlikely to have occurred … especially in light of Jesus' stated refusal to grant signs to those who sought them. Even if he had the power to perform such wonders, he specifically refused to do so. You won't find stories of the transfiguration or demonic exorcisms here, either, for the same reason.

Also not mentioned in this work are accounts of Jesus' childhood contained in several apocryphal works that sprang up in the centuries following his death. These were meant to fill in the blanks left by the four New Testament gospels, but largely depicted a petulant demigod prone to temper tantrums and rash acts of violence. In books with titles such as the Infancy Gospel of Pseudo-Matthew and the Infancy Gospel of Thomas, the following is said to have occurred:

- Jesus curses a teacher for hitting him on the head (the teacher dies).
- Jesus raises up a dead child who has fallen from a rooftop while playing with him … so the child can testify that Jesus didn't push him.
- Jesus multiplies a single grain of wheat to feed all the poor in his village.
- Idols in Egypt fall down to worship Jesus.
- Jesus enters a lioness' den and plays with her cubs.
- When Jesus' father measures a beam incorrectly and cuts it too short, Jesus miraculously lengthens it.
- Jesus makes clay pigeons on the Sabbath, for which he is criticized; he then claps his hands, and they fly away.
- When another child dares to disturb some pools of water that Jesus has created while playing, the

child is struck dead as a "son of Satan."

These stories clearly show little connection to the life and teachings of the man named Jesus as depicted in adulthood, both inside and outside the canon. For this reason, they are not included here.

Indeed, my most important condition for including certain stories connected to Jesus was that they be consistent with the themes that seemed to run through his life in the widest variety of sources: themes such as the mystery of rebirth; an aversion to hypocrisy; a tendency to do things in secret and speak in code (parables); his identity as a teacher of wisdom; his affinity with a figure he referred to as his heavenly father; and a soft spot for the poor, afflicted and persecuted.

Stories such as the account in which Jesus rescues a woman from being stoned to death and travels to India rest on tenuous historical foundations, but nonetheless are consistent with his character as presented in the majority of sources. They are included here for that reason, on the chance that they might contain a kernel of historical truth but, more importantly, because they reinforce the deeper spiritual truths Jesus himself appears to have sought to communicate during his lifetime.

I have not included accounts that purport having been gleaned from "revelations" received during meditation, trances or astral traveling, or from so-called Akashic or metaphysical records said to exist on another plane. The works of Edgar Cayce, Joseph Smith and Levi Dowling (The Aquarian Gospel) all fall into this category. Ancient texts such as the canonical Revelation of John, along with the non-canonical Revelation of Peter, Apocryphon of John and Shepherd of Hermas, among others, are further examples of this genre.

The chronology of this work is my best estimate of how the life of Jesus probably progressed, generally following the synoptic chronology while incorporating traditions from other sources (John, Thomas, Philip, Mary, the Jesus Sutras) where they seem to fit best. At times, chronology is impossible to determine. Sayings of Jesus from works that lack any biographical context themselves are used here, inserted thematically where they seem most appropriate.

I have also included a number of illustrations in the public domain.

What follows is a chapter-by-chapter collection of notes that provide added context to the narrative in the Gospel of the Phoenix, some sense of where the material came from and a few of my observations about it.

1

The first chapter of this work is my original composition and was inspired by several sources. The introductory poem is in the style of a psalm and was written to serve as short, timeless introduction to a story that takes place within the bounds of time.

It serves much the same purpose as the introduction to the canonical Gospel of John, which begins with a poetic introduction ("In the beginning was the Word …") and transitions into a more historical context.

❧

The references to the bridegroom are drawn from the Song of Solomon and the canonical gospels, while the personification of wisdom can be found in the biblical Book of Proverbs.

❧

The six ages mentioned in the second part of the chapter are patterned after the six days of creation, while the scattering of the people's tongues to the four winds is reminiscent of the Babel story from Genesis.

❧

The story of Osiris is taken from Egyptian lore. Perhaps the most complete version of the story was preserved by the Greek historian Plutarch, who was born barely a decade after Jesus' day.

჻

The final section, The Sayings of the Masters, collects and paraphrases ancient sayings from a variety of sources across the ancient world. I incorporated material from many sources to showcase both the diversity and the universal character of wisdom.

A few examples:

- "Know yourself" was inscribed on the temple of Apollo at Delphi.
- The saying that "seeing into darkness is clarity …" is taken from the Tao te Ching.
- "All war is based on deceit," is taken from The Art of War by Sun Tzu.
- "Expectation is the greatest hindrance to living," comes from the Roman philosopher Seneca.
- "In the sky, there is no distinction between east and west …" is attributed to the Buddha.
- "Boast not of the morrow, for you known not what a day may bring," can be found in the biblical Book of Proverbs.

2

The authors of the canonical gospels – especially the Gospel of Matthew – often use passages from the Hebrew scripture to preface or affirm an idea they're presenting. "As it is written in the prophet …" is a common introductory phrase. I decided to make use of this technique here. The first such reference in this section quotes Proverbs 1:20, and the reference to the wolf and the lamb is from Isaiah 11:6.

The third quotation, however, doesn't come from the Hebrew scriptures but, instead, from an Egyptian charm of protection dating to the 16th century BCE (found in P. Berlin 3027). Similarly, the reference to "the great prince of Heliopolis" comes from an ancient text titled The Contendings of Set and Horus.

ৡৢ

Several stories of Jesus' birthplace circulated in the years following his death, and I chose to include more than one here. One thing that should be said: It's unlikely that he was born in Bethlehem. The author of Luke depicts his parents traveling to Bethlehem to fulfill the conditions of a Roman census at the time of his birth. There are several problems with this story. First, there is no record of any Roman census during this period. Second, such a census would not have covered residents of Galilee, which is described as Jesus' home district and was not under direct

Roman rule at the time. And third, there's no record of any Roman census at any time requiring families to travel to the city of their ancestors, as Luke states. His purpose was doubtless to fulfill a prediction by the prophet by Micah that one destined to "rule over all of Israel" would be born in Bethlehem. Luke's narrative, however, does nothing to address the problem of Jesus' name – according to another prophecy, this one in Isaiah, it was supposed to be "Immanuel."

Jesus' hometown is matter-of-factly given as Nazareth, not Bethlehem, elsewhere in the gospels, and there's no reason to believe he was born in the "little town" of the Christmas carol.

The narrative of his birth under a palm tree can be found in the Quran (19:22-26), which was composed six centuries after Jesus' day. There is good reason to believe, however, that the tradition is far earlier. The name for the date palm in Egypt was the benu, and it was in its branches that the phoenix, or benu bird, was said to make its nest. The Greek historian Herodotus, writing in the 5th century BCE, reported hearing the story of the bird in Heliopolis, a city that plays a key role in our story. The connection of Jesus himself with the phoenix, meanwhile, dates back at least to the late 1st century.

The First Epistle of Clement, which, as mentioned above, was considered authoritative in some quarters before the canon was established, was purportedly written by Clement of Rome. This Clement is said to have been consecrated as bishop of Rome (pope) by Peter and to have served in that capacity for nearly a decade at the close of the 1st century. He wrote as follows:

"There is a certain bird which is called a phoenix, which is the only one of its kind and lives five hundred years. When the time of its dissolution draws near that it must die, it builds itself a nest of frankincense, and myrrh, and other spices, into which, when the time is fulfilled, it enters and dies. But as the flesh decays, a certain kind of worm is produced, which, being nourished by the juices of the deed bird, brings forth feathers. Then, when it has acquired strength, it takes up that nest in which are the bones of its parent, and bearing these it passes from the land of Arabia into Egypt, to the city called Heliopolis. And, in open day, flying in the sight of all men, it places them on the altar of the sun, and having done this, hastens back to its former abode."

Clement considered the phoenix's supposed existence to be a sign of the resurrection, showing that this analogy was current within at most a few decades after Jesus' lifetime. Later, however, it apparently became an embarrassment. The 9th century patriarch of Constantinople, Photios, discounted the entire epistle on the basis of its fabulous stories about the phoenix and lands beyond the ocean. (The former is no less fabulous than many stories told in the canon; as to the latter, well, we all know how that turned out.)

Early Jewish opponents of the Jesus movement quoted the Pantera story as a means of attempting to discredit Jesus' claim to be of royal lineage. Indeed, there were Roman soldiers by that name living at the time of Jesus. The grave of one, a Syrian by birth, was discovered in Germany, on the empire's northern frontier.

Questions about the legitimacy of Jesus' birth were, in fact, so widespread and pervasive that they made their way into the canonical gospels. John depicts a group of Pharisees protesting to Jesus, "We were not born of fornication" – implying that Jesus *had* been.

While it's possible there was something to this claim, it's more likely a slur designed to discredit Jesus. The identity of his supposed father as a Roman soldier would have branded his family as Roman collaborators and made them (and him) unacceptable to the Jewish nationalists who were looking for a new king to challenge Roman rule.

Who in Jesus' day would have been interested in discrediting his birth in this manner? The most likely candidates are the Herodians, who had a cozy relationship with Rome themselves and didn't want the nationalists flocking to an upstart would-be king. This is exactly what they are depicted as doing – both with Jesus and John the Baptist – throughout the gospels.

They would have been even more worried if Jesus himself were not only popular, but of Herodian blood.

৩০৫

The author of Matthew reports that Joseph and Mary fled into Egypt to avoid a murderous decree by Herod the Great: all male children two years of age and younger were to be slain. This decree was, according to the author of Matthew, an attempt to kill Jesus, whom he viewed as a rival claimant to the throne.

It should be noted that this episode, like many others in Jesus' childhood, is more difficult to verify and could easily be based on older, legendary material. For instance, it bears more than a passing similarity to Egyptian pharaoh's attempt to kill Moses in the Book of Exodus.

However, it would hardly have been out of character for Herod to order the mass slaughter of a large group of people – indeed, he is said to have done so. He ordered that a large group of people be rounded up and killed at the moment of his death, to ensure that there would be mourning in Israel at his passing – even if the mourning was not for him.

He was also notorious for having killed several potential heirs and wives whom he suspected of conspiring to seize the throne. Does this indicate that Herod believed Jesus had a legitimate claim to the throne as one of his heirs? For more information on Mary's connection to the House of Herod the Great, see my book The Phoenix Principle.

The story of Jesus' flight to and sojourn in Egypt is touched on briefly in the canonical gospels, but more extensively in other traditions, including those preserved by the Coptic Church and in a series of infancy narratives produced over the first six centuries of our era. Many of these narratives are heavy on "miracles" (some of them pretty nasty, as mentioned above) and seem to be an attempt to fill in the gaps left by the canonical material. Still, that doesn't mean the traditions they draw upon should be discounted entirely. When these obvious fabrications are removed, there remains a strong tradition that Jesus dwelt in Egypt for some period of time as a child.

Among the places he is said to have visited were the

region around Heliopolis and the Nile Delta. The former was the sacred City of the Sun, the home of the phoenix mentioned by Clement and other ancient writers. The latter region was home to the Therapeutae (literally, "healers") mentioned by the Jewish philosopher Philo of Alexandria. He describes them as a communal sect sharing all things in common and dedicating themselves to contemplation. There are points of contact with the Essenes, some Buddhist traditions and, particularly, some philosophies adopted by Jesus and his followers that are mentioned in this chapter.

If Jesus did, in fact, visit these places, it would explain his later affinity for some of the traditions and ideas that came to be central to his message. I included some of Jesus' teachings found in Matthew 6 (his discourse on the lilies of the field) at the end of this chapter to illustrate the point.

꙾

The section that refers to the rebellions and unrest in Palestine at the end of Herod's reign and thereafter is new to this edition. It is based upon accounts found in the writings of the Jewish historian Flavius Josephus.

3

I inserted some historical context and background that may have been missing from the canonical texts at the end of Chapter 2 and the beginning of this chapter by making references to the Herodian succession, and the history and geography of Galilee.

$\wp\!\sim\!\omega$

Along with Jesus' childhood, the section concerning his travels in India is the most historically problematic of this narrative. There is, nevertheless, a series of traditions placing Jesus in the East during his so-called "lost years": the period of time not covered in the canon.

The saying that compares the world to a bridge, for instance, can be found on the high gate to Fatehpur Sikri, a in the Agra district of India. It's written in Persian and dates to the first years of the 17th century, relatively recently by historical standards.

The Ten Methods are drawn from the so-called Jesus Sutras, a series of Chinese-language sayings that date from the 7th century mission of Alopen, considered the first Christian missionary to reach China. These aphorisms cannot be traced to Jesus himself with any certainty, but the same can be said for virtually all sayings that have been attributed to him over the centuries. These were chosen because they appear to blend elements of Christian, Buddhist and Taoist philosophies in a manner that presents

Jesus' teachings in a unique yet consistent way.

Other material here is drawn from a document said to have been transcribed by a 19th century Russian aristocrat and journalist named Nicholas Notovich, based on an original he reported finding at a Tibetan Buddhist monastery. Today, his story is considered highly questionable, and most scholars dismiss it as an outright fabrication. As mentioned in the introduction, the Jesus story, even within the canon itself, is a patchwork of accounts and traditions that vary widely in terms of historical reliability. The Notovich account is probably no more or less likely to be accurate than the closing verses of Mark or the account of the woman caught in adultery that was added at the beginning of John 8.

There is a persistent tradition that Jesus spent time in India, which is in itself noteworthy. Still, I suspect that most stories of this sort are based in the realms of poetry and speculation, rather than history, and they are included here largely because they seem compatible with Jesus' message as presented elsewhere.

Some of the similarities between Jesus' own philosophy as conveyed in other writings and various elements of Buddhism are presented in this chapter. Whether this indicates Jesus spent time in India, received these traditions from another source or simply adopted ideas of his own that were consistent with some elements of Buddhism is difficult to determine. But the traditions themselves are noteworthy and are included here for that reason.

4

The Hebrew term for carpenter, *naggar*, can also mean a learned man. Considering the fact that Jesus was referred to as a rabbi, the latter definition seems far more likely.

ഴ∂

The similarities between the names of Jesus' brothers and some of his closest disciples seem too close to be coincidence. The fact that his brother James took leadership of the movement after Jesus' death would seem to confirm this, as does the tradition that Judas' nickname "Thomas" (the twin) identified him in some traditions as Jesus' own twin brother.

Another epithet Iscariot, applied to Judas, identifies him as a member of an elite group of assassins known as the Sicarii or "knife-wielders." It was their custom to sneak up on their targets, knives concealed beneath their cloaks, and strike suddenly, killing them.

This would indicate that an element of Jewish nationalism was present in Jesus' movement and, even more significantly, within his own family. The identification of Judas as an assassin and Simon as a member of the radical nationalist movement known as the Zealots would have made Jesus a target. This is perhaps one reason for his extreme caution in disguising his movements and speaking in code, interpreting the meanings of what he said only to trusted associates.

The author of Mark describes one incident in which Jesus has drawn a large crowd and is told that his mother and brothers have arrived to see him. His answer appears specifically designed to distance himself from them: "Who are my mother and my brothers?" This could well have been because he didn't want to associate with known radicals – at least not when such a large number of people was present.

Jesus' association with known anti-Roman nationalists was problematic for him and can make it difficult for us to interpret his actions. Was he a revolutionary himself who was simply being careful to avoid attracting the attention of the authorities, or was he a sage whose family sympathized with the Jewish nationalists but did not endorse them himself? The answers aren't always clear. This text adopts the latter view; my previous book, The Phoenix Principle (written before The Gospel of the Phoenix but published afterward), suggests that there's an argument to be made for the former position, as well.

❧

The story of Honi the Circle drawer, drawn from the Hebrew Mishnah, identifies him as a figure similar to John the Baptist: a prophet who operated outside the priestly tradition and was feared as something of a "loose cannon" who could back up his words with power.

The carob tree, mentioned in the story of Honi, is closely associated with John the Baptist, as well. According to tradition, John ate carob beans, and these beans even came to be known as "St. John's bread." The word carob bears a certain similarity to Kher-heb, an Egyptian priest responsible for reciting religious texts and presiding over funerary rites, as well as cherub, a specific type of heavenly creature. More information on this can be found in The Phoenix Principle.

ৡৱ

When Jesus came up out of the water at his baptism, he was told, "On this day have I begotten you." This is the wording in the apocryphal text known as The Gospel of the Hebrews, quoting directly from Psalms 2:7. The synoptic gospels (Matthew, Mark and Luke), however, omit this language in describing Jesus' baptism, thereby buttressing the idea of Jesus' divine birth … as opposed to a symbolic anointing or "begetting."

The theological motive for changing the language of the Psalm is clear, and it provides ample reason for preferring the original version preserved in The Gospel of the Hebrews. Ironically, the baptism's significance as a second birth is minimized as a result. Jesus clearly referred to the two births and may well have viewed his baptism as a second birth.

The birth symbolism is made apparent by the presence of the dove, symbolic not only of the entrance to the birth canal but also long associated with the mother goddess Astarte. The declaration that "on this day have I begotten you" would have made this explicit but was abandoned for the reasons stated above.

5

The material in this chapter is largely taken from the canonical gospels, but the closing quotes are from the Gospel of Thomas, a collection of sayings that some believe was compiled before the four works included in the Bible. They show Jesus referring to the kingdom as a spiritual entity rather than a realm to be established by political means or force of arms.

The Gospel of Luke contains a shorter version of the saying, but the version included here is more poetic and more powerful.

ॐ

I chose not to include many miracle stories in this volume; I wanted to focus on Jesus' role as a sage and teacher, rather than getting sidetracked by debates over apparently "supernatural" abilities.

Jesus himself spoke of an "evil and idolatrous" generation seeking confirmation through signs and wonders. As in this chapter, I made a few exceptions with regard to accounts of healings, which may not have been miraculous at all. As mentioned previously, Jesus most likely had some extensive knowledge of healing techniques through his contact with the Therapeutae.

6

This account of John's confrontation with Herod Philip is contained in the Slavonic text of a work called The Jewish War. The original version of this extensive volume was produced in the late 1ˢᵗ century by Flavius Josephus, an ethnic Jew who originally fought with the nationalist resistance against Rome but later switched sides and supported the empire.

The Slavonic version surfaced in Russia in the 19ᵗʰ century and includes some additional material concerning John the Baptist and Jesus. The latter can be quickly discounted as an attempt to insert information about Jesus into material where it was (embarrassingly, for Christians) lacking, but the information of John does not appear to designed to accomplish this. Although many have dismissed it, this material may contain the kernel of truth from an earlier tradition and is included here for this reason.

❦

The remainder of the material in this chapter combines information on the trial and execution of John from four sources: the canonical synoptic gospels, as well as another work of Josephus, The Antiquities of the Jews, which he wrote as a comprehensive history of the Jewish people.

The synoptics tell the familiar story of how Salome asked for John's head on a platter after performing a dance before the drunken tetrarch Herod Antipas (one of Herod the Great's sons, who had inherited a portion of his kingdom).

The author of Luke mentions in passing that John had rebuked Antipas "because of Herodias, his brother's wife, and because all the evil things that Herod had done." But Josephus supplies the details: that Antipas had sought to divorce his own wife – the daughter of the neighboring Arab king Aretas – in order to marry his own brother Philip's wife. Herodias, perhaps enticed by the fact that Antipas was more powerful and ambitious than his brother, accepted Antipas' proposal.

Aretas' daughter, learning of the plan, went to the city of Machaerus on the border between Antipas' lands and her father's, and thence fled to her father's kingdom. It was also to the fortress at Machaerus that John was sent, and there that he was imprisoned at the time of his death.

Did Aretas' daughter attempt in some way to conspire with John? There is no way to know. But what is known is that John had built a following so substantial that Antipas viewed him as a threat. According to Josephus, he didn't give this order merely because Salome requested it. Instead, he did so because he feared that John's "strong influence over the people might lead to a revolt, for they appeared ready to do anything that he should advise."

Aretas subsequently went to war against Antipas, destroying his army, and John's followers viewed this as divine judgment against the tetrarch for having John put to death.

It seems likely that all these events were tied up together: Antipas' betrayal of Aretas' daughter; John's imprisonment and subsequent death; the machinations of Herodias and her daughter Salome; the events at Machaerus; and the subsequent war between Aretas and Antipas.

Salome's name, interestingly, later appears among Jesus' followers. She is one of the women mentioned by the author of Mark as having witnessed the crucifixion and brought spices to anoint Jesus afterward. She is also mentioned among the followers of Jesus in the Gospel of Thomas and the extracanonical Gospel of the Egyptians.

She was not the only woman associated with Jesus who had ties with Herod's household. A follower of Jesus' named Joanna was married to a man named Cuza, who was in charge of Antipas' household.

ভৎ

Herod Antipas is referred to in this text as Antipas, rather than Herod, to avoid confusion. The canonical texts all call him Herod, but as a result, he's often confused with his father, whose name was also Herod. The elder Herod ruled as client king to the Roman emperor until his death in 4 BCE. At that time, his kingdom was split up into four parts, two of which (including Jerusalem) went to his favorite son, Archelaus, while the other two were divided between two other sons, Herod Antipas and Herod Philip. Antipas became tetrarch of Galilee and Philip took the lands to the northeast, beyond the Jordan River. Archelaus was eventually removed from office and replaced by a Roman prefect, the office to which Pontius Pilate was appointed in 26 CE.

ക∼

Mary Magdalene is often believed to have come from a town named Magdala, but there is nothing to suggest this. The Aramaic word magdala (Hebrew migdol) meant simply "great" or "tower." No other woman among Jesus' followers is identified with a place name, which would seem to indicate that magdala was a title referring to her high stature within Jesus' movement.

The reference to Jesus kissing Mary often on the mouth is from The Gospel of Philip. It demonstrates that the persistent identification of Mary as Jesus' wife is not simply a sensational idea that has sold a lot of novels for one Dan Brown, but an ancient tradition probably based on fact.

7

The well-known story of Jesus' temptation by Satan in the wilderness corresponds well with the ancient story of Horus' battles with Set. The desert was Set's domain. The quotations here are from the Book of Victory Over Set, the Egyptian text of a ritual performed at the temple of Osiris in Abydos.

Osiris was considered the heavenly father in Egyptian lore, and Jesus took the role of his earthly son and heir, Horus – the reigning king or messiah. Set was the rival bent on enticing him to forsake the way of his heavenly father and thus controlling him.

The Egyptians believed that the pharaoh would ascend to the heavens, specifically to the constellation of Osiris, Orion. At this point, they believe the dead pharaoh personified Osiris, just as he had personified Horus in his life on Earth. He literally became one with his father in heaven. This sort of language is attributed to Jesus at various points in his public life and indicates he identified with the Egyptian myth.

8

The poetic saying that includes the phrase "the sun is my warmth in winter, and my candle is the moon" is taken from Islamic tradition.

❧

Simon is called a Pharisee in some instances, a leper in others; the logical conclusion is that he was both.

❧

The "sinful woman" who is depicted in Luke as anointing Jesus' feet with perfume and her own tears is traditionally associated with Mary Magdalene, out of whom he was said to have case seven demons. The anointing described in this chapter is said to have taken place at a village called Bethany.

It can hardly be coincidence that another scene set in Bethany involves a woman named Mary who is content to sit at Jesus' feet.

There is plenty of reason to believe that Mary Magdalene was, in fact, Jesus' wife. The Gospel of Philip and in The Gospel of Mary both indicate that Jesus loved Mary more than his male disciples. Not only does she kiss his mouth in the former passage, but she kisses his feet at Bethany in the canonical texts.

In anointing Jesus, both in this instance and again

following his crucifixion, she is acting as someone who has a right to perform one of the most intimate functions imaginable. According to the author of John, she also joined Jesus' mother and his aunt in attendance at his crucifixion, suggesting that she, like they, was a family member.

There's much more to this, and I've addressed it in far greater depth in The Phoenix Principle.

ৡৡ

Jesus compared himself to the bridegroom, a title identified with the legendary King Solomon. It was to him that the poetic scripture known as the Song of Songs (or Song of Solomon) was attributed, a work that describes a bridegroom's passion for his beloved.

By doing this, Jesus suggested a strong affinity for this role: "Would you compel the guests of the bridegroom to fast while he is among them? Yet the time will come when the bridegroom shall be removed from their presence, and in those days will they fast." It would have made little sense for him to refer to himself in such terms if it were merely allegorical. He is clearly identifying with the figure of Solomon, who was known more than anything for two things: his wisdom and his identity as a bridegroom (he reportedly had hundreds of wives).

The text from the Book of Proverbs chosen in this chapter may have served as a model for Jesus' own wedding. It brings together the themes of wisdom, wine and celebration in a short section of text, providing a virtual blueprint for a wedding feast.

It is just this sort of wedding feast that is described in the narrative that speaks of the wedding in Cana, an event that more than one observer has remarked seems to be Jesus' own. He is in charge of providing the refreshments, indicating a position of authority at the event.

The turning of water into wine identifies Jesus as the heir of Osiris, the green-faced king of vine and verdure. It is no coincidence that the Greek god of the vine, Dionysus, was said to have turned water into wine, which supposedly sprang forth from a fountain at Andros once a year. (Also worth noting: Herodotus and others equated Dionysus with Osiris centuries before the time of Jesus.)

§∞℘

The story of Sarah, the daughter of Jesus and Mary Magdalene, comes from French tradition. The connection of Mary with France (Gaul) is strong and very old; the legend says she gave birth to a daughter, Sarah, in Egypt and that they sailed from there to Gaul with Joseph of Arimathea. Further legends claim Joseph went on from there to Great Britain. The fact that Sarah is called "the Black" could indicate that Jesus, Mary or both had some Egyptian/African blood. A brief addition to this segment was made for this edition.

9

The Samaritans seem to have had a profound effect on Jesus. Like the lepers, the poor and others on the margins of society, they had been cast aside and were avoided as "unclean" and theologically incorrect. Jews traveling from south to north (or vice versa) would typically go the long way around to avoid Samaritan territory.

In the account of the Samaritan woman at the well, familiar from John 4, Jesus indicates that sharing the most basic of resources, water, is far more important than questions concerning a person's ethnic background, where one should worship or how many times someone might have been married. In one single act, Jesus sweeps aside social, religious and ethnic barriers. In their place he proposed an attitude of reverence in "spirit and truth" – the "living water."

In his parable of the good Samaritan, related elsewhere, he seemed to indicate that those who had been marginalized were more likely to be attuned to the troubles of those around them than were those who believed they were righteous, such as the Pharisees whose hypocrisy he so roundly criticized.

∽●∽

"He who knows the father and the mother shall be called the son of a harlot." This saying is taken from The Gospel of Thomas. It would seem to indicate a lack of acceptance for those who regarded the masculine and feminine divine principles as equally important. Certainly, this would have been the case in Jerusalem, where the cult of Yahweh tolerated no other god save the single masculine god of Israel.

ৡৡ

The sayings near the end of this chapter are taken from the Jesus Sutras.

ৡৡ

The section on the disciples' vision is new to this edition. It is an abridged version of a short discussion that appears in the Gnostic Gospel of Judas.

10

"Even did my mother, the divine spirit, take me by a single hair on my head and bring me to the great mountain called Tabor." This saying is one of seven preserved by the church father Origen from The Gospel of the Hebrews.

Ancient tradition equated Jesus' mother with the holy spirit. The symbol of the dove, as mentioned, was the symbol of the goddess Astarte. In the Hebrew scriptures, wisdom was often depicted as feminine in the Hebrew scriptures and as the consort of both kings such as Solomon and the Hebrew god himself. As time went on and the priesthood of Yahweh consolidated its power, acknowledgement of the corresponding female principle was first downplayed and ultimately proscribed altogether. Asherah poles, honoring the ancient Ugaritic mother goddess known as the "Queen of Heaven" (the same title accorded to Isis and, later, Jesus' mother, Mary) were cut down and thrown into the flame.

Jesus, however, appears to have acknowledged and sought to restore this feminine principle through the symbolism of the bridegroom and his consort, the recognition of women's equal status within his movement and various sayings such as this. Unfortunately, such sayings were subsequently suppressed and excluded from canonical writings by religious leaders who claimed Jesus' authority but failed to follow his example.

Most of this chapter has been drawn from canonical texts.

11

The scene in which the disciples see a baby nursing at its mother's breast and his subsequent comments are taken from The Gospel of Thomas. So are the questions and answers concerning when the disciples will enter into their rest and how their end will come, which appear slightly later in this chapter.

ভৢৢ

"All nature, and everything there is, and every earthly creature – all these exist in and with one another. For the nature of earthly things is to dissolve into the root of their own being." This saying is taken from a fragmentary Gnostic text titled The Gospel of Mary (Magdalene).

ভৢৢ

"Some rulers wanted to deceive a man ..." A parable from The Gospel of Philip. The source is the same for the saying that "truth did not enter the world naked, but came adorned in forms and images."

12

The four principles shared as part of Jesus' teachings in this chapter are taken from the Jesus Sutras.

෫෧෪

Some forms of Christianity have been used, historically, as a means of reducing women to a secondary or even subservient status. This has been seen, especially, in interpretations of Paul's epistles. By contrast, a broad spectrum of material concerning Jesus appears to indicate a much more egalitarian view.

Jesus' view that it was wrong to divorce a woman simply by giving her a piece of paper would have been empowering in a time when men often treated their wives as servants whom they could dismiss without cause. This particular saying is found in the canonical text, but such attitudes are affirmed elsewhere, as well.

The Gospel of Thomas contains the quote, attributed to Peter, urging Jesus to dismiss Mary Magdalene from their presence. The Gospel of Mary includes an account of a similar interaction, also included here, that was said to have driven Mary to tears. The scene continues with another among them (identified in the original text as Levi) admonishing Simon as a hot-tempered individual who has dared to oppose Jesus directly: "If the master made her worthy, who are you to reject her?"

ᔆᖇᓍ

The section titled Teachings of the Disciples is a brief selection of sayings from the epistles of James (concerning wisdom) and Paul (concerning the parts of the body and the excellence of love). The last of these is among the most profound and poetic passages in the canon.

13

The framework for the narrative is taken from the Gospel of John, the only place where this account is found. A related parable concerning a rich man and a beggar by the name of Lazarus is found in the Gospel of Luke.

৽৽৵

Lazarus was not a name, but rather the title of the role an individual played in the healing ritual that involved a symbolic death and rebirth. This was a theme commonly emphasized within the Jesus movement. In this case, the title was that of Osiris or Al Asar, the dying-and-rising god of the Egyptians whom Jesus regarded as his heavenly father.

Both Simon and "Lazarus" are depicted as owners of a home who host a feast at which Jesus is present, and both are closely associated with Mary/the sinful woman. The fact that Simon the Leper was clearly sick (with leprosy), and Lazarus is also identified as sick is another point of contact. For more on the identification of Simon the Pharisee/Leper as Lazarus, see The Phoenix Principle.

৽৽৵

"I have come for you that I might clean you, cleanse you and revive you. Rise up and live!" This quote comes from the Pyramid Texts, which describe the raising of

Osiris. The reference to Horus dispelling the evil that was upon Osiris for four days is also found in the Pyramid Texts. In this ceremony, Jesus is playing the role of Horus, an office he claimed for himself generally speaking as heir to the throne of heaven.

14

The connection between the story of Balaam's donkey and the story of Jesus is one I noticed while researching this book. I included it as a poetic point of contrast between the story of Balaam, whose donkey refused to move when waylaid by an angel, and that of Jesus', whose ass bore him willingly toward Jerusalem.

The ass was also a totem animal of Set, along with the hippopotamus. Jesus' decision to ride into Jerusalem on the back of such an animal may have indicated that he identified himself as having spiritually conquered the forces of chaos Set represented.

⁌⁍

The account of Jesus' arrival in Jerusalem is traditionally called The Triumphal Entry. I have cast it here as The Humble Entry to emphasize the sense of the prophet Zechariah's declaration, referred to by the author of Matthew: "Behold, your king comes to you humbly, riding on a donkey."

The quote provided here, "... let him who has power renounce it ..." is attributed to Jesus in the Gospel of Thomas.

15

The account of Jesus driving the money-changers out of the temple is contained near the beginning of John but near the end of the other canonical gospels. It makes far more sense in the latter context, serving as grounds for Jesus' arrest.

❦

The brief scene of Jesus at the dye works of a man named Levi is taken from the Gospel of Philip.

❦

The story of the man born blind, set at the Pool of Siloam, is taken from the Gospel of John. For more about the possible significance of this story, see The Phoenix Principle.

16

The incident involving the crowd's mistreatment of the crone and Jesus' injunction to respect women are taken from the document purportedly discovered by Nicholas Notovich in Tibet. The scene is included here because it is consistent with Jesus' teachings, but I chose to introduce it with the phrase "it is said that" to indicate the disputed status of this and other sayings from that source.

The comparison of Eve and Lilith is my own observation.

☘

The famous story in which Jesus comes to the aid of a woman accused of adultery is found in the Gospel of John. It is not, however, contained in most of the oldest manuscripts and is widely considered to be a later insertion. Its original source is unclear. Whether it comes from a different tradition or is a later invention, it is consistent with Jesus' overall teachings concerning forgiveness and is included here for that reason.

☘

The author of John tells the story of Jesus' encounter with critics who took pride in being sons of Abraham and accused him of having a demon. They also, interestingly, accused him of being a Samaritan (the equivalent of an ethnic slur in that day). The latter charge probably stemmed from Jesus' willingness to associate with Samaritans. Interestingly, he did not answer it, perhaps indicating he didn't feel the identification was an insult. He did, however, rebut the charge of demon possession with his famous saying that "a house divided is sure to fall." In doing so, he addressed one of the problems inherent in a dualist world view that depicts positive and negative forces in perpetual conflict. By contrast, Jesus seems to have been arguing that all things came from a single source, and that any kingdom that operated against its own interests was self-defeating.

᠀᠀

The well-known diatribe of "woes" against the Pharisees shows a side of Jesus that reflects his impatience with hypocrisy. Together with his actions in driving the money-changers out of the temple, it shows a passion for justice and fairness that both complements and contrasts with other well-known sayings, such as his injunction to "turn the other cheek."

These episodes indicate that Jesus was no pushover; rather, he was a complex individual whose defense of the poor and afflicted could move him to act against those who sought to perpetuate injustice.

17

This chapter marks the beginning of the story's climax, which I introduce with the idea that Jesus was seeking to fulfill his role as Horus and undergo a ritual "second birth" as Osiris, the heavenly father. In its aftermath, he would "ascend to the father."

One possible implication of this is that Jesus was ill, and he knew it. Simon/Lazarus, likewise, had been ill, but Jesus had reassured his followers that Lazarus' illness "will not end in death." Something interesting then occurs: Lazarus reportedly dies. This indicates one of two possibilities. Either Jesus was wrong in predicting the illness would not end in death of he was right and Lazarus was still alive when he was put in the tomb.

The latter seems more plausible. Lazarus' "death" was part of a ritual death and rebirth, and he never really died at all.

The story of Lazarus may provide some insight into Jesus' own death. Like Lazarus, he may well have been sick, but unlike Lazarus, it's possible he suspected his sickness *would* end in death. Under these circumstances, he would have wanted to complete the death-and-rebirth ritual before he was dead – before it was time for him to "ascend to the father."

Simon/Lazarus is never depicted as "ascending to the father, which would indicate he survived.

✈

"Cleave the wood, and I am there. Lift a stone, and there you will find me" is a quotation from the Gospel of Thomas.

❧

Jesus' rebuke to Peter is traditionally translated as including a reference to the proper name "Satan." I have translated it instead to include the translation of the word satan: adversary. This translation has always seemed to make more sense. Peter was opposing Jesus and therefore was acting like an adversary; Jesus wasn't mistaking him for a malevolent celestial being.

❧

The doctrine of original sin did not originate with Jesus, but rather with Paul. It was Paul who depicted Jesus' death as a sacrifice meant to satisfy divine "judgment" against the entire human race for an offense supposedly committed by a single ancestor (Adam).

Not only did this idea have no precedent in Jesus' teachings, it was explicitly excluded by the Hebrew scriptures. Various excerpts from those texts were used to illustrate this idea. The prophet Hosea had declared, "I desire mercy, not a sacrifice" (Hosea 6:6). The longer quotation in this section ("He who kills a bull is as if he slays a man ...) is from Isaiah 66:3. The texts concerning bribery come from the Proverbs and, again, from Isaiah.

Not quoted here is Ezekiel's declaration that men are

responsible for their own acts, not the acts of their fathers or others in their family:

"The word of the lord came to me: What do you people mean by quoting this proverb in the land of Israel: 'The parents eat sour grapes, and the children's teeth are set on edge'? As surely as I live, the lord declares, you will no longer quote this proverb in Israel. For everyone belongs to me, the parent as well as the child; both alike are mine. The one who sins is the one who will perish."

The concept of original sin, depicted almost as a disease transmitted from generation to generation, simply has no place in light of such a declaration. It was at odds with the prophetic tradition of personal transgression and responsibility, and Jesus himself never proposed anything like what Paul taught.

18

Jesus had made arrangements in advance with followers inside Jerusalem to prepare a place for the Passover feast, and these arrangements were largely unknown to the disciples who were traveling with him. This becomes clear in the gospels when he tells his companions to find a man carrying a jar of water, who will then take them to a large guest room where the feast is to be held.

The water jar is meant to serve as a sort of secret signal, and is consistent with Jesus' practice of communicating in code, speaking in parables whose meanings were hidden to outsiders ... but which he later explained to his associates in private. His reference to a furnished room and plans for the feast indicate that extensive preparations had been made: preparations known only to Jesus and his contacts in Jerusalem, not to most of his traveling companions.

∽∾

The tradition that James vowed to fast until Jesus' mission was complete can be found in a fragmentary text called the Gospel of the Hebrews. A handful of excerpts from this text were preserved in early quotations from it, but the full document has been lost.

∽∾

"What you must do, do quickly." Jesus' enigmatic

statement to Judas has often been interpreted as a sign that Jesus knew, supernaturally, that Judas was destined to betray him. A far simpler (and more plausible) explanation is that he was telling Judas to do something that had been discussed ahead of time. Just as Jesus had made arrangements ahead of time to have a man with a jar meet his companions on their entrance to the city, he had made arrangements with Judas to prepare for what lay ahead. In sending Judas out without explanation, he trusted that plans discussed ahead of time (without the knowledge of the others present at the feast) would be carried out.

∽∾

The irony that Judas, who was carrying out Jesus' instructions, was later branded as a betrayer, while Peter, who repudiated him, was later lauded as the first great leader of his movement is not to be missed. Ultimately, neither was true. Numerous writings, both canonical and extrabiblical, identify Jesus' brother James as his successor and the next great leader of his movement. He is clearly depicted as such by the author of Acts.

∽∾

The famous saying "pride goeth before a fall," mentioned here, can be found in the sixteenth Proverb.

∽∾

The serpent's ancient role as a symbol of wisdom and rebirth has largely been forgotten; instead, the creature has been cast as a treacherous purveyor of temptation. This second view is largely based on its supposedly villainous role in the Genesis account. Yet even in that text, the older traditions lurk just beneath the surface. The serpent is described as the most cunning of all creatures, indicating its role as a keeper of wisdom. It is also associated with an offer of life ("you surely shall not die"). The idea of lifting up a symbol of wisdom and life can also be linked to the caduceus, a short staff entwined by two serpents and carried by the god Hermes in Greek mythology. It endures today as the symbol of medicine.

19

Pontius Pilate was often depicted in early Christian literature as a sympathetic figure who later testified that Jesus had risen from the dead and blamed the Jewish leaders for his death. Documents such as the Acts of Pilate and a letter purportedly from Pilate to Claudius embedded in the apocryphal Acts of Peter and Paul shifted the responsibility off of Pilate's shoulders and instead blamed "the wickedness of the Jews."

The supposed letter to Claudius has little, if any value. Pilate is known to have committed suicide during the reign of the Emperor Caligula, who preceded Claudius in that position; Pilate, therefore, would not have been alive to provide testimony to the latter emperor.

Instead, the so-called Pilate literature represented a pernicious strain of anti-Semitic bigotry traceable in part to the Gospel of Matthew, whose author quoted the crowd before Pilate as demanding Jesus' crucifixion with these words: "His blood be upon us and our children." (This quotation is paraphrased in Chapter 20 of the present work.) The author of John, likewise, repeatedly refers to "the Jews" as Jesus' enemies.

The picture of Pilate as somehow sympathetic to Jesus, however, would have seemed absurd to anyone who knew him. He is known from other historical accounts to have been ruthless and without sympathy for those who dared to oppose either Rome or him personally. Philo of Alexandria said he was "by nature both unyielding and relentless," being noted for his "vindictiveness and raging temper." These qualities are illustrated by his actions during the incidents recounted here: the first regarding Caesar's standards, and the second involving a proposed aqueduct to Jerusalem. These accounts are not found in the canon, but rather in the histories of Philo and Josephus.

ೲ

The charge that Jesus was born of fornication was implicit in an earlier confrontation with the Pharisees in the Gospel of John. Its inclusion in this scene is based on a document called the Gospel of Nicodemus or the Acts of Pilate, which was produced later but contained this same accusation.

ೲ

Pilate's decision to send Jesus off to the Antipas no doubt involved a desire to conveniently dispose of a politically problematic issue without a major scene that could lead to an uprising. If a local authority such as Antipas were to deal with the Jesus "problem," it would prevent Rome from being directly implicated and becoming a target for popular discontent.

Antipas, however, was apparently too smart to take the bait. (Jesus is said to have called him, "that fox.") He reportedly dressed Jesus in a purple robe and sent him back to Pilate. The message was clear: Jesus was being accused of setting himself up as a king (purple being the royal color) and, as a result, was a direct threat to the empire. As such, the empire's appointed representative was the proper person to decide his case … and that person was Pilate.

∽≪

The name "Barabbas" meant "Son of the father," a role Jesus had claimed for himself in relationship to his heavenly father. In some Greek and Syriac manuscripts of Matthew, Barabbas is even referred to as "Jesus Barabbas." When the crowd was demanding that Pilate release Barabbas, they were really calling for *Jesus* to be released.

20

The first quotation in this chapter, which ends with the declaration, "And my days shall be as the days of the Phoenix," is found in the Book of Job from the Hebrew scriptures.

ॐ

The Book of Going Forth by Day is the original name of the Book of the Dead, an ancient Egyptian funerary text produced some 1,500 years before the time of Jesus.

ॐ

The canonical texts provide various accounts in which one or two figures are present at the tomb of Jesus. The version from Mark is used here because it is both the oldest and the simplest. The author of Matthew refers to a single angel, and the author of Luke to two men in white whose clothing shone like lightning.

Mary's encounter with Jesus is described most fully in the Gospel of John, where she plays the same role ascribed to Isis in ancient tradition: that of the grieving consort searching for the body of her beloved, Osiris … who like Jesus had died and was destined to rise again.

ॐ

The proclamation of Osiris is taken from Chapter 64 of the Egyptian Book of the Dead.

❧

Didymus Judas Thomas is identified as the full name of Jesus' disciple in the Gospel of Thomas. Thomas' name is also given as Didymus by the author of John. "Didymus" was Greek for "twin," and the name Thomas carried the same meaning in Aramaic.

Whose twin was he? According to one tradition, he was the twin to none other than Jesus himself. For instance, a Gnostic text discovered at Nag Hammadi titled the Book of Thomas the Contender contains a quote in which Jesus identifies Thomas as "my twin and true companion." If Judas was, in fact, Jesus' twin brother, it would go a long way toward explaining why Jesus trusted him to carry out the "betrayal" that led to his arrest.

❧

The declaration that Jesus did everything in "a mystery, a baptism and an anointing" is taken from the Gospel of Philip.

❧

The death-and-rebirth ritual probably wasn't nearly as grueling or excruciating as the gospels indicate. For one thing, the assertion that Jesus' legs were broken seems untenable if we are to believe that he was capable of walking – as the gospels indicate he was – afterward. His side may have been ritually pierced with a spear, but care would have been taken not to do any major damage.

The narrative leaves as an open question how long Jesus survived after the crucifixion. The likelihood is that he didn't live long. As indicated above, he may very well have been sick before the ritual, and any time at all hanging from a cross (even in a brief ritualized setting) would have been taxing on his body.

According to the author of Acts, Jesus remained among his followers forty days before ascending into heaven and thus taking on the role of the Osiris and becoming one with the heavenly father. The figure is almost certainly symbolic (forty was often used in this sense, both when measuring days, as in the flood, and years, as in the description of the Hebrews' wandering in the wilderness after their flight out of Egypt).

The absence of any historical references to Jesus after the crucifixion, coupled with James' ascension to leadership of the movement shortly thereafter, would seem to argue against his survival for an extended period of time.

Palestine, 1ˢᵗ century CE

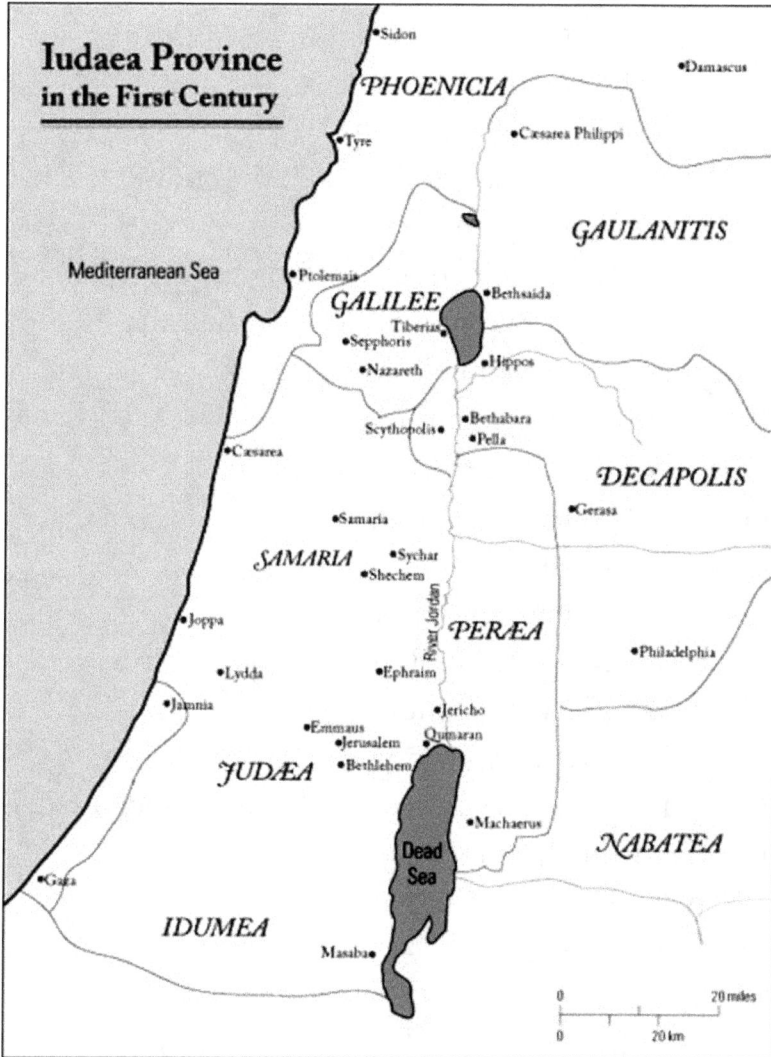

Sources

Antiquities of the Jews (Flavius Josephus)
    also: Slavonic version
Book of the Dead (Egyptian)
De Iside et Osiride (Plutarch)
De Vita Contemplativa (Philo of Alexandria)
Epistle of James (Canonical)
First Epistle of Clement to Corinth (Apocryphal)
First Epistle of Paul to Corinth (Canonical)
Gospel of the Ebionites (Apocryphal)
Gospel of the Egyptians (Apocryphal)
Gospel of the Hebrews (Apocryphal)
Gospel of John (Canonical)
Gospel of Judas (Gnostic)
Gospel of Luke (Canonical)
Gospel of Mark (Canonical)
Gospel of Mary (Gnostic)
Gospel of Matthew (Canonical)
Gospel of Nicodemus/Acts of Pilate (Apocryphal)
Gospel of Philip (Gnostic)
Gospel of Thomas (Gnostic)
Histories (Herodotus)
Hosea (Hebrew)
Infancy Gospel of Pseudo-Matthew (Apocryphal)
Infancy Gospel of Thomas (Apocryphal)
Isaiah (Hebrew)
Jeremiah (Hebrew)
Job (Hebrew)

Jesus Sutras (Apocryphal)
Jewish War (Flavius Josephus)
Life of Issa (Apocryphal)
Mishna (Hebrew)
Proverbs (Hebrew)
Psalms (Hebrew)
Pyramid Texts (Egyptian)
Thomas the Contender (Gnostic)
Zechariah (Hebrew)

Praise for other works by the author

"The complex idea of mixing morality and mortality is a fresh twist on the human condition. ... **Memortality** is one of those books that will incite more questions than it answers. And for fandom, that's a good thing."

— Ricky L. Brown, Amazing Stories

"Punchy and fast paced, **Memortality** reads like a graphic novel. ... (Provost's) style makes the trippy landscapes and mind-bending plot points more believable and adds a thrilling edge to this vivid crossover fantasy."

— Foreword Reviews

"Whether a troubled family's curse or the nightmarish hell created by a new kind of A.I., the autopsy of a vampire or Santa's darker side ... Provost's sure hand guides you down gloomy avenues you do not expect."

— Mark Onspaugh, author of The Faceless One and Deadlight Jack, on **Nightmare's Eve**

"**Memortality** by Stephen Provost is a highly original, thrilling novel unlike anything else out there."

— David McAfee, bestselling author of 33 A.D., 61 A.D., and 79 A.D.

"Profusely illustrated throughout, **Highway 99** is unreservedly recommended as an essential and core addition to every community and academic library's California History collections."

— California Bookwatch

"As informed and informative as it is entertaining and absorbing, **Fresno Growing Up** is very highly recommended for personal, community, and academic library 20th Century American History collections."

— John Burroughs, Reviewer's Bookwatch

Stephen H. Provost

The author writes about American highways, mutant superheroes, mythic archetypes and pretty much anything he wants. A journalist, historian, philosopher and novelist, he lives on the Central Coast of California. And he loves cats. Read his blogs and keep up with his latest activities at stephenhprovost.com.